"ANC

CALLING

"ANOTHER JESUS" CALLING

How Sarah Young's False Christ is Deceiving the Church

WARREN B. SMITH

Expanded Second Edition

Mountain Stream Press
Magalia, California

"Another Jesus" Calling
© 2013 Warren B. Smith
Expanded Second Edition, 2016
First edition published by Lighthouse Trails Publishing

Mountain Stream Press
P.O. Box 1794
Magalia, CA 95954

Publisher's Cataloging-in-Publication Data
Smith, Warren B.
  ANOTHER JESUS CALLING : How false christs are entering the church : through contemplative prayer / Expanded second edition / Warren B. Smith.
    pages cm
  Includes bibliographical references.
  ISBN 978-0-9978982-9-3 (softbound : alk. paper) 1. Christianity and other religions--New Age movement. 2. Young, Sarah, 1946- Jesus calling. I. Title.

Printed in the United States of America

Dedication

For all those
who have a love of the truth

For if he that cometh preacheth another Jesus, whom we have not preached, or if ye receive another spirit, which ye have not received, or another gospel, which ye have not accepted, ye might well bear with him.

—2 Corinthians 11:14

Contents

NOTE
TO THE
READER (2013)

IN APRIL 2013, I received a phone call just prior to traveling to Canada to speak at a prophecy conference. Two women from the La Crete, Alberta conference were concerned about a best-selling book titled *Jesus Calling*. The author, Sarah Young, had published personal messages she said she received from Jesus Christ. The two women had an uneasy feeling about the book and wanted me to look into it. I was aware of the book but didn't realize it had become so popular. So the next day when I went to our local Christian bookstore, I was surprised to see *Jesus Calling* piled high in two stacks on the floor in front of a shelf where it was already fully stocked. It was obviously *very* popular.

I noticed that *Jesus Calling* came in a variety of sizes and styles. There was the standard compact, rust-colored, hardcover edition that I held in my hands. A small egg-shaped picture of an inviting outstretched hand was in the middle of the front cover. The title read, *Jesus Calling: Enjoying Peace in His Presence.* And a line at the top of the front cover read, "Devotions for Every Day of the Year." Another edition of the same book had what was called a "leather look," while another had a genuine cowhide cover. There was a sage-colored version, a pink-colored version, a special edition for teens, as well as a *Jesus Calling* (*Bible Storybook*) for children. Prominently featured on a display rack were numerous copies of the *Jesus Calling Devotional Bible.* Off to my left were more Sarah Young titles—*Dear Jesus, Jesus*

Today, and *Jesus Lives*. I would later discover there was a *40 Days with Jesus* booklet and a *Jesus Calling Devotional Calendar*. The copy of *Jesus Calling* I was holding in my hands informed me that the book was "now available for the iPhone, iPod Touch, iPad, and all Android devices." It was also available on an audio CD. When I asked the clerk how many copies of *Jesus Calling* they had sold, he replied "thousands."

I said, "Really?"

He said, "Really."

The copyright page informed me that *Jesus Calling* was originally published in 2004, and I would learn that over time it eventually became the number one best-selling book for Christian retail in 2010. It has already sold over nine million copies. And as I write, it continues to be the #1 best-selling book in Christian bookstores, as well as #3 on the *Wall Street Journal's* best-seller list for *all* non-fiction books—secular and Christian.

In the "Introduction" to *Jesus Calling*, Sarah Young said she had been inspired to receive personal messages from "Jesus" after reading a book called *God Calling*. I remembered *God Calling* because it was a book I had when I was involved with New Age teachings. I found it troubling that Sarah Young had been inspired by a metaphysical book like *God Calling*. So that afternoon after purchasing *Jesus Calling* at the Christian bookstore, I also bought a copy of *God Calling* at a used bookstore. I would later find out that *God Calling* was being featured along with *Jesus Calling* in another local Christian bookstore.

The following day while traveling to Alberta, I started reading *Jesus Calling*. I learned that Sarah Young, the daughter of a college professor, majored in philosophy at Wellesley College and later earned her master's degree in counseling and biblical studies at Covenant Theological Seminary in St. Louis. Young related how she and her third-generation missionary husband served two four-year terms in Japan doing church planting work. Returning to the United States after the second term in Japan, she obtained a further degree in counseling at Georgia State University while her husband was employed at a local Japanese church in Atlanta. Later, after moving to Australia and while also continuing her counseling practice, Young assisted her husband in planting the first Japanese church in Melbourne. It was in Australia that she first read *God Calling*.

By the time I arrived in Northern Alberta, I had finished reading both *Jesus Calling* and *God Calling*. Because of my concern about what I had just read, I made *Jesus Calling* the subject of one of my talks at the prophecy conference. I later felt that my concerns needed to be covered more completely, which is why this book was written.

Because *Jesus Calling* contains personal "messages" that Sarah Young says were given to her by Jesus Christ, it is important to determine if these messages were really from Jesus. Are they consistent with the teachings of God's Word? Is anything new or questionable being subtly introduced? In short, can we trust *Jesus Calling* as a godly devotional book?

Having been formerly involved in the New Age movement, I became immediately concerned when I read the book. It was troubling for me to see a number of New Age practices and concepts being presented as completely normal for Christians. Even more troubling, there were no warnings or disclaimers about what was being introduced. By the end of the book, *Jesus Calling* and its "Jesus" had subtly and not so subtly introduced occult/New Age channeling, spiritual dictation, creative visualization, meditation, divine alchemy, co-creation with God, and *practicing the presence* like it was everyday Christian fare. New Age terms and concepts were brought into the messages like they were no big deal. And added to this were indirect references to a pantheistic poet and two classic New Age books, along with a hearty endorsement of *God Calling*—the channeled book that inspired Sarah Young to try and receive her own personal messages from Jesus.

The unusual use of language by the "Jesus" of *Jesus Calling* was also disturbing. It seemed to run the gamut from "everyday Joe" language to strange word choice, unwarranted flattery, worldly clichés, repetitive phrases, disparaging comments, and not-so-subtle mockery. All in all, *Jesus Calling* seemed to be an obvious attempt by our spiritual Adversary to get an even further foothold inside the Christian church.

While I was surprised that Sarah Young's devotional had become such a huge best-seller in the Christian marketplace, I was not completely surprised. Deceptive occult/New Age teachings are swallowing up much of what calls itself Christian these days.

In this book, I have done my best to raise some of my questions and concerns. I am sure my conclusions will upset a great many people who are devoted to *Jesus Calling*. Obviously, what you do with these conclusions is completely up to you. But I couldn't imagine not bringing what I discovered to your attention. Hopefully, you will consider what I have presented here.

Warren B. Smith

NOTE TO THE READER (2016)

SOON AFTER THE original edition of *"Another Jesus" Calling* was published in 2013, Sarah Young and her publisher, Thomas Nelson, changed, altered, and deleted a number of key problematic areas in *Jesus Calling* that I had exposed in *"Another Jesus" Calling*. These changes were made in the new printings of their book that were sent to bookstores without any explanation or apology regarding the revisions made to Sarah Young's original text. Their obvious quick-fix editing caused understandable confusion as a number of my footnotes in *"Another Jesus" Calling* would no longer have any point of reference in these new revised printings of *Jesus Calling*. A special 10th anniversary edition of *Jesus Calling* in 2014 made even more changes in their ongoing effort to do damage control for their seriously flawed book.

In this new expanded edition of *"Another Jesus" Calling*, four new appendices have been added to help clear up some of the confusion created by Sarah Young and her editorial team. These new appendices include "Changing *Jesus Calling*: Damage Control For A False Christ," "The New Age Implications of *Jesus Calling*," "10 Scriptural Reasons Why *Jesus Calling* is a Dangerous Book," and "Serious Concerns about Sarah Young's *Jesus Calling Devotional Bible*."

May God give us the discernment and wisdom to spot deceptive false Christs when they arise in our midst—and may God enable us to see how some authors and publishers are all too willing to sacrifice truth and integrity to perpetuate the sales of their best-selling books.

WARREN B. SMITH

PROLOGUE

SOMETIMES WHEN I am far from home and attempt to send an e-mail, a notice pops up on the computer screen from my e-mail provider. Because I am in a different location, the provider needs to verify my identity by asking a few questions. The same thing happens with my credit card company. When I travel to a distant city and make a purchase, someone from the credit card company will sometimes contact me to make sure the purchase wasn't made by someone who has stolen my card and is pretending to be me.

There are a growing number of companies that will monitor for the possible misappropriation of your identity. They watch for unusual activity with the use of your name in regard to credit cards, etc. If anything seems to be the least bit suspicious, they immediately get in touch with you. Generally, we don't take offense with their questions because most of us agree it is better to be safe than sorry.

IDENTITY THEFT

IDENTITY theft is a harsh reality in today's world. That's why we have security codes and passwords as well as various organizations that will monitor your affairs. They are there to protect your identity. Identity theft serves as a useful analogy. When Jesus was asked by His disciples what would be the sign of His return and the end of the world, He responded by saying that *His* identity would be stolen. He warned that because *many* would claim to be Him, many would be deceived:

And as he sat upon the mount of Olives, the disciples came unto him privately, saying, Tell us, when shall these things be? and what shall be the sign of thy coming, and of the end of the world? And Jesus answered and said unto them, Take heed that no man deceive you. For many shall come in my name, saying, I am Christ; and shall deceive many. (Matthew 24:3-5)

Later in that same passage, Jesus emphasized the widespread extent of the theft of His identity. He said that if it were possible, even the elect would be deceived:

For there shall arise false Christs, and false prophets, and shall shew great signs and wonders; insomuch that, if it were possible, they shall deceive the very elect. Behold, I have told you before. (Matthew 24:24-25)

FALSE CHRISTS

IN the last several decades, false Christs have gone from the utterly obvious to the deceptively subtle. When I lived in San Francisco years ago, there was a local character named "Jesus Christ Satan." Wearing lipstick and a long flowing robe, he paraded around the city barefoot, waving a huge United Nations flag while cradling a small dog under his arm. When Jesus warned of false Christs, He wasn't just talking about people like "Jesus Christ Satan," Waco's David Koresh, or the "Reverend" Jim Jones of the People's Temple. These false Christs were merely caricatures that seemed to render all false Christs unbelievable. And this is precisely the kind of stereotype that Satan wants Christians to associate with the term "false Christ"—too obvious and unbelievable for most people.

What our spiritual Adversary doesn't want people to know is the much more subtle deception going on in the world and in the church *right now*—a deception in which voices purporting to be "Jesus," "God," and the "Holy Spirit" are speaking directly to people through books, as well as in their quiet times of meditation, contemplative prayer, and yes—"practicing the presence." And it is a deception, which brings us back to what the real Jesus was warning about in Matthew 24 regarding the end times.

Identity theft—particularly the theft of Jesus' identity—has been an incredibly well orchestrated ongoing process. Our spiritual Adversary's plan from the start has been to cleverly establish a counterfeit Christ that gradually introduces *new* revelations and *new* teachings and a New Age/New World Religion solution to a troubled world desperately looking for answers. His patient but steady attack on the church has increased greatly over the past several decades. According to Scripture, his deceptive plans will culminate with the greatest identity theft of all time. He will present himself to the world *as* Christ. Literally fulfilling the meaning of the term *Antichrist*, he will come in the name of Christ but will actually oppose Christ and everything the true Christ stands for.

A "WONDERFUL" DECEPTION

AS a New Ager, sitting on the floor of the Either/Or Bookstore in Hermosa Beach, California, in 1983, I read Johanna Michaelsen's stunning book *The Beautiful Side of Evil*. The sobering and enlightening account of this former New Age follower contained severe warnings about spiritual deception. She warned how spiritual experiences that come in the name of Jesus are not necessarily from Him—experiences that can feel wonderful and uplifting when they are actually deceptive and evil.

Johanna described how she accepted Jesus Christ as her Lord and Savior in college but became spiritually deceived because she had no real understanding of the Bible. She didn't know the Scriptures warned about seducing spirits (1 Timothy 4:1) and that we need to test the spirits (1 John 4:1-3) to make sure that what we are experiencing is really from God.

After graduating from college, Johanna began working as an assistant to an occult psychic surgeon in Mexico City who was performing miraculous healings on a wide variety of people. Johanna thoroughly believed that she was serving God by doing this. Much of this conviction was based on the personal relationship that she *thought* she had with Jesus Christ but would later realize was not *the true* Jesus Christ at all. Johanna was in frequent contact with this "Jesus" during her meditations, devotions, and quiet times. But when certain events caused her to question some unusual things that were happening with the psychic surgeon and the psychic healings, she decided to take a leave of absence from her spiritual work.

JOHANNA MICHAELSEN AT L'ABRI

JOHANNA traveled to Europe to get a fresh perspective. While visiting her sister in Florence, Italy, her sister suggested she go to L'Abri—a Christian community in the Swiss Alps run by Francis and Edith Schaeffer. After talking with L'Abri staff and reading the Gospel of John and John's first epistle, Johanna reached a point where she felt convicted to pray and ask God for wisdom (James 1:5). She earnestly prayed that if she was being deceived she wanted God to let her know; but if she was not being deceived, she planned on returning to Mexico City to resume work with the psychic surgeon. God answered her prayer and made it clear that she was being deceived, and she later confronted her two spirit guides, "Jesus Christ" and "Mamacita." Using the Bible's test for spirits, she entered the meditation "laboratory" she had been taught to visualize in her "mind's eye" where she often met with "Jesus." Addressing this "Jesus," she put him to the Bible's test:

> "You are not the Jesus in the Bible, are you," I challenged the figure of "Jesus" which stood before me in the shadows. There was no reply. His eyes were closed. Mamacita stood close by him. "Then I command you, in the Name of Jesus Christ of Nazareth, tell me: Do you believe that Jesus Christ is God uniquely incarnate in human flesh?" A violent flash—as though from a

powerful bomb, brought the walls of my amethyst and gold laboratory down all around me. When I looked up, my counselors had vanished.[1]

Thanks to Johanna Michaelsen's book *The Beautiful Side of Evil*, and a series of circumstances in my own life that brought the deceptiveness of evil to the surface, I came to realize the "Jesus" I had been following in the New Age movement was not the true Jesus Christ but actually one of the false Christs the true Jesus was warning about in Matthew 24, Mark 13, and Luke 21. I share my story in my book *The Light That Was Dark: From the New Age to Amazing Grace*. Thank God the Bible provides us with a means for confronting the spirit world when it tries to deceive us. We are not left to our own intuition and subjectivity. We are not left to our own devices or those of our spiritual Adversary. There is a scriptural way to test the spirits (see 1 John 4:1-3; James 1:5) and make sure that we are not giving heed to the voice of a counterfeit—to "another Jesus" that comes calling.

SARAH YOUNG AT L'ABRI

AFTER graduating from college, and before completing her master's degree, Sarah Young described how she first experienced the presence of "Jesus" while staying at a French branch of Francis and Edith Schaeffer's L'Abri Christian community. Young had gone to L'Abri after reading Francis Schaeffer's book *Escape from Reason*. In the "Introduction" to *Jesus Calling*, she wrote:

> One night I found myself leaving the warmth of our cozy chalet to walk alone in the snowy mountains. I went into a deeply wooded area, feeling vulnerable and awed by cold, moonlit beauty. The air was crisp and dry, piercing to inhale. Suddenly I felt as if a warm mist enveloped me. I became aware of *a lovely Presence, and my involuntary response was to whisper, "Sweet Jesus."* This utterance was

totally uncharacteristic of me, and I was shocked to hear myself speaking so tenderly to Jesus. As I pondered this brief communication, I realized it was *the response of a converted heart;* at that moment *I knew I belonged to Him.* This was far more than the intellectual answers for which I'd been searching. This was a relationship with the Creator of the universe.[2] (emphasis added)

A year after Sarah Young's initial encounter with the presence of "Jesus" at L'Abri, she encountered the presence again in an Atlanta, Georgia, hotel room in the midst of a personal crisis:

I knelt beside the bed in that sterile room and felt an overwhelming Presence of peace and love come over me. *I knew* Jesus was with me and that He sympathized with my heartache. This was *unquestionably* the same "Sweet Jesus" I had met in the Alps.[3] (emphasis added)

A logical assumption is that this "same 'Sweet Jesus'" is the same "Jesus" that provided Sarah Young with the messages she eventually published as *Jesus Calling.*

TWO OUTCOMES

TWO young women traveled to L'Abri Christian communities run by Francis and Edith Schaeffer with two very different outcomes. Johanna Michaelsen's visit to L'Abri resulted in the *abandonment* of her "Jesus" presence when she realized he wasn't the true Jesus Christ. Yet Sarah Young's visit to L'Abri resulted in the immediate *acceptance* of her "Jesus" presence, which she just "knew" was Jesus Christ.

THE NEED FOR DISCERNMENT

THE Bible challenges believers to be watchful and discerning regarding the ongoing activities of our spiritual Adversary. We are not to be ignorant of his devices (2 Corinthians 2:11). We need to study the Word of God and to be very careful about what we read, hear, and take into our hearts and minds (2 Timothy 2:15). We are to be like the Bereans who "searched the scriptures daily" to make sure the things they were being told were *really* "so" (Acts 17:11). We should be examining ourselves to make sure we are still in the faith (2 Corinthians 13:5). And we are told to "try the spirits" of those who purport to speak for God (1 John 4:1-3). We need to make sure the *voice* we are being asked to heed is not the voice of a counterfeit "stranger" (John 10:4-5).

GOD CALLING

BECAUSE *Jesus Calling* has become an international best-seller and is influencing so many people, it is important to carefully examine Sarah Young's book. To do this, we must first take a look at *God Calling*—the book that originally inspired her to receive messages from "Jesus" and to eventually have them published as *Jesus Calling*. Sarah Young has described *God Calling* as "a treasure to me,"[4] a "treasure" that has sold ten million copies with its *God at Eventide: Companion Volume to God Calling* and is a best-seller in its own right.

What was it about the "Jesus" in *God Calling* that engaged Sarah Young at such a profound life-changing level? And what is it that we can learn about Sarah Young and *Jesus Calling* by having a better understanding of *God Calling*? I distinctly remembered this book from my days in the New Age, and after reading it again thirty or so years later, I have outlined ten of my many concerns.

PART ONE

GOD CALLING

TEN CONCERNS

1

CHANNELED BOOK FROM JESUS?

od Calling is a channeled book that was delivered through
an occult process known as spiritual dictation. As previously
mentioned, I had this book on my bookshelf with all my other
New Age/metaphysical books when I was involved in the New Age
movement many years ago.

GOD CALLING IS a collection of messages presented in the form
of a daily devotional. The messages were channeled through two
women and could just as easily have been titled *Jesus Calling* because
they were said to be dictated by Jesus Himself. The "Introduction"
to *God Calling* states:

> Not one woman but two have written this book; and they
> seek no praise. They have elected to remain anonymous
> and to be called "Two Listeners." But the claim which they
> make is an astonishing one, that their message has been

given to them, to-day, here in England, by The Living Christ Himself.[1]

A promotion on the front page of *God Calling* describes the book as "a mine of spiritual treasures." And Sarah Young states in the "Introduction" to *Jesus Calling* that *God Calling* "became a treasure to me" and inspired her to see if she, too, could receive messages from Jesus.[2] In an online interview with the Christian Broadcasting Network, Sarah Young also stated:

> My journey began with a devotional book (*God Calling*) written in the 1930s by two women who practiced waiting in God's Presence, writing the messages they received as they "listened."[3]

In the *Encyclopedia of New Age Beliefs, God Calling* is cited as an example of a channeled New Age book "replete with denials of biblical teaching."

This book that inspired Sarah Young is addressed in the *Encyclopedia of New Age Beliefs*—a Christian work published in 1996 by Harvest House Publishers. The encyclopedia contains a thirty-four page chapter that warns about channeling. It explains that channeling is a form of mediumship and "is a practice forbidden (Deuteronomy 18:9-12)."[4] This Scripture specifically warns that "a consulter with familiar spirits" is an abomination unto the Lord. Also in this encyclopedia, under the heading titled "Impersonations and Denials of Christianity," *God Calling* is cited as an example of a channeled New Age book "replete with denials of biblical teaching"[5] as it "subtly encourages psychic development and spiritistic inspiration under the guise of Christ's personal guidance . . . and often misinterprets Scripture."[6]

God Calling is an example of what occult practitioners refer to as spiritual dictation. This is when a spiritual entity conveys information from the spirit world to a willing "channel" or "listener." The channel usually speaks or writes what the spirit dictates. Many New Age teachings have been delivered in this way. In *God Calling*, "Jesus" told the Two Listeners—

> You do well to remember your friends in the Unseen.[7]

> I cannot bless a life that does not act as a channel.[8]

> Be channels both of you.[9]

And while also seeming to denounce the practice of mediumship, "Jesus" told the Two Listeners to *be mediums*:

> No man should ever be a medium for any spirit, other than Mine.[10]

This kind of New Age/metaphysical language is found throughout *God Calling* and its follow-up book *God at Eventide: Companion Volume to God Calling.*

2

Permeated With New Age Terminology

Much of *God Calling* contains New Age language and teachings that are being incorporated into the church.

> And the LORD said, Behold, the people is one, and they have all one language; and this they begin to do: and now nothing will be restrained from them, which they have imagined to do. (Genesis 11:6)

APPARENTLY NAIVE TO the danger of occult spiritual dictation, Sarah Young was spiritually inspired by reading *God Calling* and embarked on a journey that would soon parallel that of the Two Listeners. Rather than being discerned as the occult book it is, *God Calling* instead led Sarah Young to seek her own dictated messages from "Jesus," which millions of people are now reading in *Jesus Calling*.

So much of *God Calling* is permeated with metaphysical/New Age terminology and thinking. The following is just a sampling of the occult/New Age terms that continually jump out at the reader—Universal Spirit,[1] Supreme Being,[2] Divine Powers,[3] Great Divine Heart,[4] Divine Forces,[5] Spirit Forces,[6] God-Power,[7] spiritual plane,[8] channels,[9] Spirit-consciousness,[10] heart-consciousness,[11] Spirit Sounds,[12] Spirit-communication,[13] Divine Mind,[14] Secret of Prosperity,[15] Law of Supply,[16] Law of Discipleship,[17] Sonship,[18] spiritual level,[19] path of initiation,[20] order out of chaos,[21] soul-balance,[22] oneness,[23] and many others.

What many Christians do not realize is that the deceptive spirit world is thoroughly capable of weaving Christian terminology and verses from the Bible in and around metaphysical/occult terms and teachings. Mixing truth with error, they often deliver their messages through inner voices, whispers, spiritual dictation, automatic writing, channeling, and impressions in the name of "God," "Jesus," and the "Holy Spirit"—especially when they want to deceive Christians or those interested in learning about Christ. The apostle Paul warned that these seducing spirits would deceive Christians in the latter times:

> Now the Spirit speaketh expressly, that in the latter times some shall depart from the faith, giving heed to seducing spirits, and doctrines of devils. (1 Timothy 4:1)

GOD'S UNIVERSAL SPIRIT?

God Calling opens the door to relativistic truth and universalism. The "Jesus" of God Calling said:

> It is only the work of the Universal Spirit—My Spirit, that counts.[1]

> Remember that Truth is many-sided.[2]

THE TRUE JESUS *is* the "truth" (John 14:6), and He is *not* "many-sided." This "many-sided" false teaching opens the door to New Age Universalism. In New Age teachings, a "many-sided" Christ is all things to all people and all religions. In the Two Listeners' follow-up book to *God Calling* titled *God at Eventide: Companion Volume to God Calling* and under the heading "All One," "Jesus" states:

> You are to know no difference of race, colour or *creed*. One is your Father, and all ye are brethren.

This is *the Unity I came to teach—Man* united with God and His great family. Not man alone, seeking a *oneness* with God alone. See God the Father with His great world family, and, as you seek union with Him, it must mean for you attachment to His family, His other children.[3] (emphasis added)

And the "Jesus" of *Jesus Calling* seems to agree:

I have called each of My children to a different path, distinctly designed for that one. Do not let anyone convince you that his path is the only right way. And be careful not to extol your path as superior to another's way.[4]

We *are* to love all people regardless of race, color, and creed, and love them right where they are at. But that does not mean there is no difference between people's various religious and spiritual beliefs (creeds). There are huge differences—radical differences. The Bible is clear that Jesus did *not* teach a broad Universalism, but rather a very narrow way:

Enter ye in at the strait gate: for wide is the gate, and broad is the way, that leadeth to destruction, and many there be which go in thereat: Because strait is the gate, and narrow is the way, which leadeth unto life, and few there be that find it. (Matthew 7:13-14)

GOD "IN" EVERYONE?

The "Jesus" of *God Calling* teaches that God is "in" everyone. New Age leaders have described this teaching as foundational to the coming New World Religion.[1]

BECAUSE THE "JESUS" of *God Calling* teaches that God is "in" everyone "at the centre of every man's being," this should be enough for believers to close up the book and stop reading. This teaching is foundational to the New Age/New Spirituality/New Worldview. Apparently, Sarah Young knew very little about this heretical teaching or she would not have trusted the "Christ" that taught this to the Two Listeners:

> True it is, I wait in many a heart, but so few retire into that inner place of the being to commune with Me. Wherever the soul is, I am. Man has rarely understood this. I *am* actually at the centre of every man's being, but, distracted with the things of the sense-life, he finds Me not.

Do you realize that I am telling you *truths,* revealing them, not repeating oft-told facts. Meditate on all I say. Ponder it. Not to draw your own conclusions, but to absorb Mine.[2]

In each of you too, remember there *is God.* That God I reverence and submit to, though I and My Father are one. So as man grows more and more like My Father in Heaven I bring to our friendship a reverent, tender Love. I see as no man can see *the God in you.*

It is always given to man to see in his fellow man those aspirations and qualities he himself possesses. So only I, being really God, can recognize *the God in man.* Remember this, too, in your relation to others.[3] (emphasis added)

The Bible makes it clear that God does not naturally and universally reside "in" every person. While man *is* made in God's image, the true Jesus Christ said we "must" be born again (John 3:5-8) and *then* the Holy Spirit will be sent to us (John 14:16-18). If God were already "in" everyone as *God Calling* teaches, then no one would need the Holy Spirit to be sent to them, and no one would need to be born again. And if this were the case, no one would need Jesus Christ in order to be saved. It would simply be save yourself by going within to the God within. This is the teaching of the New Age/New Spirituality. The Bible, however, teaches that God is *not* in everyone.

But Jesus did not commit himself unto them, because he knew all men, And needed not that any should testify of man: for he knew what was in man. (John 2:24-25)

[V]erily every man at his best state is altogether vanity. (Psalm 39:5)

Put them in fear, O LORD: that the nations may know themselves to be but men. (Psalm 9:20)

Now the Egyptians are men, and not God. (Isaiah 31:3)

[F]or I am God, and not man. (Hosea 11:9)

Remember the former things of old: for I am God, and there is none else; I am God, and there is none like me. (Isaiah 46:9)

Thus saith the Lord GOD; Because thine heart is lifted up, and thou hast said, I am a God, I sit in the seat of God, in the midst of the seas; yet thou art a man, and not God, though thou set thine heart as the heart of God. (Ezekiel 28:2)

There is a tremendous push by our spiritual Adversary to get humanity to accept this New Age teaching that God is "in" everyone, and it is being taught in many churches by pastors who still consider themselves to be evangelical. This teaching has emerged everywhere and most believers are unaware of its tremendous deceptive significance. But man is *not* God.

Name it
& Claim it

The "Jesus" of *God Calling* introduces unbiblical, hyper-charismatic, new agey, "name it and claim it" "health and wealth" teachings.

HERE ARE SOME of the statements found in *God Calling*:

I, who could command a universe—I await the commands of My children.[1]

Command Your Lord. [2]

Claim big, really big things now. Remember nothing is too big.[3]

Claim the unclaimable.[4]

Claim My power.[5]

Think health—health comes. The physical reflects the mental and spiritual.[6]

Be not afraid, health and wealth are coming to you both.[7]

To dwell in thought on the material, when once you live in Me,—is to call it into being. So you must be careful only to think of and desire that which will help, not hinder, your spiritual growth. The same law operates too on the spiritual plane.[8]

The Bible teaches that we don't demand, command, affirm, and declare that *our* will be done. We ask that things be done according to God's will. We are to pray not *my* will Lord but *thy* will be done (Matthew 6:10). The "name it and claim it" teachings that have come into the church through many Christian leaders, as well as through books like *God Calling*, are very similar to the *creative visualization* and *create your own reality* teachings that are at the very heart of the New Age movement. "Name it and claim it" in occult/New Age teachings is better known as the Law of Manifestation. Another occult law somewhat connected to this is the Law of Supply. The Law of Supply is repeatedly referenced in *God Calling*.[9] God abhors occultism. We are not to operate under occult law. Scripture warns, "For all that do these things are an abomination unto the LORD" (Deuteronomy 18:10-12).

We are to operate under the law of God. *God's* will be done, not *my* "name it and claim it" will be done. God does sometimes still give people their request for their own will to be done, but Psalm 106:15 says it best:

And he gave them their request; but sent leanness into their soul.

EXPERIENCE REPLACES GOD'S WORD

*G*od *Calling* elevates spiritual experience over the Word of God which opens the door to spiritual deception.

IN THE "INTRODUCTION" to *God Calling*, the Two Listeners placed their spiritual experience with "Jesus" over the Bible itself. Regarding what they considered to be their special role of receiving dictated information from "Jesus," they wrote:

> We felt all unworthy and overwhelmed by the wonder of it, and could hardly realize that *we* were being taught, trained and encouraged day by day by Him personally, when millions of souls, far worthier, had to be content with guidance from the Bible, sermons, their Churches, books and other sources.[1]

And the "Jesus" of *God Calling* put it even more bluntly:

> Know no theology. Know Me.[2]

When man ceased to commune with his God simply and naturally, he took refuge in words—words. . . . Rely less on words.[3]

The New Age "God" and "Christ" have said much the same thing. According to the "Jesus" of the channeled *Course in Miracles*—which Oprah Winfrey has consistently promoted since 1992:

A universal theology is impossible, but a universal experience is not only possible but necessary.[4]

Words will mean little now. We use them but as guides on which we do not now depend. For now we seek direct experience of truth alone.[5]

"God" speaking through New Age leader Neale Donald Walsch said:

Listen to your *feelings*. Listen to your Highest Thoughts. Listen to your experience. Whenever any one of these differ from what you've been told by your teachers, or read in your books, forget the words. *Words are the least reliable purveyor of Truth.*[6]

There is a continual emphasis in *God Calling* and in New Age teachings to rest, meditate, abide, sit, be still, be calm, and *experience* God's presence, which always seems to take precedence over reading, studying, and *knowing* God's Word. The situation is ripe for spiritual deception when the Word of God is minimized and spiritual experience is raised above it.

All scripture is given by inspiration of God, and is profitable for doctrine, for reproof, for correction, for instruction in righteousness: That the man of God may be perfect, thoroughly furnished unto all good works. (2 Timothy 3:16-17)

JESUS NEEDS US MORE THAN WE NEED HIM?

esus Christ, the Creator of the Universe—Who gives "to all life, and breath, and all things" (Acts 17:25)—would never say that He needs us more than we need Him.

SCRIPTURE TELLS US:

For by him were all things created, that are in heaven, and that are in earth, visible and invisible, whether they be thrones, or dominions, or principalities, or powers: all things were created by him, and for him: And he is before all things, and by him all things consist. (Colossians 1:16-17)

Neither is worshipped with men's hands, *as though he needed any thing*, seeing he giveth to all life, and breath, and all things. (Acts 17:25, emphasis added)

But, in *God Calling*, "Jesus" states:

I need you more than you need Me.[1]

The true Jesus Christ is the Creator, and our Lord and Savior. He can do anything He wants, and He certainly does not need us—His created—to accomplish anything. We didn't even exist yet when Jesus Christ simply spoke all of creation into existence. In regard to the true Jesus Christ, the "I need you more than you need me" quote is wholly untrue.

On the other hand, a false "Jesus" *does* need us more than we need him. Without us, a false "Jesus" would be and have nothing. It is the followers of a false "Jesus" that give this false "Jesus" a sense of "trueness." In regard to a false "Jesus," the "I need you more than you need me" quote is wholly true.

No less theologically skewed is also the following quote from *God at Eventide: Companion Volume to God Calling*. It, too, reveals the utter falseness of this "Jesus":

> You must stand as a sinner with a sinner before you can save him. Even I had to hang between two thieves to save My world.[2]

Regarding the true Jesus Christ, Scripture tells us "he was manifested to take away our sins; and in him is no sin" (1 John 3:5).

There are many other quotes from the "Jesus" of *God Calling* and its *Companion Volume* that are also revealing, but these two examples give quite a picture of the nature of this "Jesus." Think about this when reading the following unbiblical statement of this "Jesus":

> So, My children, union with Me is the one great overwhelming necessity. All else follows so naturally, and union with Me may be the result of just consciousness of My Presence. . . .

When man ceased to commune with his God simply and naturally, he took refuge in words—words. Babel resulted.[3]

Suffice it to say that contrary to this quote of "Jesus" in *God Calling*, the true Jesus Christ actually said:

If a man love me, he will keep my words: and my Father will love him, and we will come unto him, and make our abode with him. (John 14:23)

He that is of God heareth God's words: ye therefore hear them not, because ye are not of God. (John 8:47)

Scripture is clear that communion with the true God is *inseparable* from His words. Only a *false* "Jesus," who needs us more than we need him, would counsel us to overlook these words in order to have communion with *him*.

But continue thou in the things which thou hast learned and hast been assured of, knowing of whom thou hast learned them; And that from a child thou hast known the holy scriptures, which are able to make thee wise unto salvation through faith which is in Christ Jesus. (2 Timothy 3:14-15)

8

New Truth & New Revelation?

According to the "Jesus" of *God Calling*, "Man's thoughts of Me need revolutionizing."[1] To accomplish this, he will introduce new truths and new revelations.

IN *GOD CALLING*, "Jesus" states:

> For you, My children, I will unlock the *secret treasures* hidden from so many.[2] (emphasis added)

> I am revealing so much to you. Pass it on. Each Truth is a jewel.[3]

> Seek to find a heart-home for each Truth I have imparted to you. *More Truths* will flow in.[4] (emphasis added)

And in *God at Eventide*, "Jesus" promised:

Life holds in store more wonderful possibilities than you can sense as yet, and ever, more and more, as you go on, will further possibilities reveal themselves.[5]

. . . where fresh visions are spread out before you, and where I can teach you *My Secrets* of those Heights.[6] (emphasis added)

In that quiet realm of the Spirit, where dwell all who are controlled by *My* Spirit, there can all secrets be revealed, all Hidden-Kingdom-Truths be shown and learned.

Live there, and *Truth* deeper than all *knowledge* shall be revealed to you.[7]

So there must be much silence in our companionship, because you are not yet able to bear *all the Wonder-Truth I long to impart.*[8] (emphasis added)

Only those in close touch with Me, inspired by My Spirit, *infected* by My Love, impregnated with My Strength, retain a resilience of being and *receptivity to new Truth.*[9] (emphasis added)

The very real danger of spiritual experiences is that they can be used to introduce *new truths* and *new revelations*. This is what the New Age is founded on, and the experiential "truths" and "revelations" of the New Age have been in the process of "infecting" the church for many years now. As these *new truths* and *new revelations* supplant God's Word, they definitely revolutionize man's thoughts of Jesus Christ—which opens the door to embracing "*another* Jesus."

> For if he that cometh preacheth another Jesus, whom we have not preached, or if ye receive another spirit, which ye have not received, or another gospel, which ye have not accepted, ye might well bear with him. (2 Corinthians 11:4)

9

THE NEW AGE & PSALM 46:10

here are repeated references in *God Calling* to Psalm
46:10—"Be still, and know that I am God"—and a continuous
encouragement to "Cultivate silence"[1] and to meet "Jesus" in that
silence.

YET *GOD CALLING* issues no warnings about seducing spirits
(1 Timothy 4:1) that often wait in the silence to converse with naive
seekers of God's presence. The seekers, in so doing, open a door into
the evil spirit realm and into deception.

When I was involved in the New Age, we sometimes repeated
Psalm 46:10 before meditating. The verse was recommended by
many New Age leaders as a way of entering the silence and ini-
tiating contact with God. Today, this same recommendation is
given by many Christian leaders. And, in fact, one church leader
who does so even endorses a book by New Age leader Deepak
Chopra in which using Psalm 46:10 is also recommended. This
endorsement of Lead Like Jesus co-founder Ken Blanchard can

be found in Chopra's book, *The Seven Spiritual Laws of Success: a Practical Guide to the Fulfillment of Your Dreams*. In this book, Chopra emphatically declares that in order to know God one *must* meditate. He underscores his New Age call to meditation by citing Psalm 46:10 and putting practical New Age meaning on the single word "Be." He writes:

> The very real danger of spiritual experiences is that they can be used to introduce new truths and new revelations.

Practicing silence means making a commitment to take a certain amount of time to simply *Be*. [2]

In the Bible is the expression, "Be still, and know that I am God." This can only be accomplished through meditation. [3]

Likewise, Ken Blanchard, in his own book *Lead Like Jesus*, cites Psalm 46:10 and urges readers to focus on the single word "Be." And like Chopra, Blanchard also puts an obvious New Age emphasis on this word "Be." Blanchard writes:

> Before we send people off for their period of solitude, we have them recite with us Psalm 46:10 in this way:

> *Be still and know that I am God.*

> *Be still and know.*

> *Be still.*

> *Be*. [4]

This idea of simply "being" was at the heart of my New Age experience. However, I came to understand that just "being" can result in an overly relaxed, falsely confident, passive state of mind where trusting souls do not think to test the spirits. As a result, many of us learned the hard way that what we thought we were hearing and experiencing and feeling was not from God at all.

As will be explained in Section 11 of Part Two, Psalm 46:10 has *nothing* to do with being still and meditating on God. It was a call to obedience, *not* to meditation and practicing the presence.

NEW AGE CHRISTIANITY?

T here is no such thing as New Age Christianity. But there are many people who think of themselves as New Age Christians, and there are many New Age books filled with Christian terms, concepts, Bible verses, and Bible references—books like *God Calling*.

GOD CALLING IS a New Age book that is framed in Christian terminology. Much like the Oprah-endorsed *A Course in Miracles* that was also said to be spiritually dictated by "Jesus Christ," *God Calling* is more of a transitional New Age book to gradually move Christians out of biblical Christianity and into a counterfeit New Age Christianity. But New Age Christianity is an oxymoron in that the concept is a fundamental contradiction of terms. *God Calling* was truly exposed for what it is when its "Jesus" stated that God is "at the centre of every man's being"—"wherever the soul is, I am."[1] This alone defines *God Calling* as a New Age book because this teaching is foundational to the New Age/New Spirituality/New Worldview, and "a little leaven" leavens the whole book. Scripture describes this perfectly:

> Ye did run well; who did hinder you that ye should not obey the truth? This persuasion cometh not of him that calleth you. A little leaven leaveneth the whole lump. (Galatians 5:7-9)

CONCLUSION

MANY of us had the book *God Calling* when I was involved with the New Age movement, and much more can be said about this metaphysical book that purports to be Christian. Suffice it to say that it weaves Christian terminology in and around some extremely unbiblical statements and concepts. So for Sarah Young to describe this book as "a treasure to me" and to recommend it so enthusiastically to her millions of readers was hard to comprehend. That is, of course, until I actually read her book *Jesus Calling*. In many ways, Sarah Young's book picks up where *God Calling* leaves off. Part Two of this book will outline some of the concerns any believer should have about *Jesus Calling*.

> Many of us learned the hard way that what we thought we were hearing and experiencing and feeling was not from God at all.

Come now, and let us reason together, saith the LORD.—Isaiah 1:18

PART TWO
JESUS CALLING

TWENTY CONCERNS

1

Inspired By a Channeled New Age Book

Sarah Young's journey to writing *Jesus Calling* started with *God Calling*—a channeled New Age book delivered through the occult process of spiritual dictation. The fact that she called this book "a treasure" should give any discerning Christian reason to immediately question the authenticity of her book and her "Jesus."

IN THE "INTRODUCTION" to *Jesus Calling*, Sarah Young wrote about her involvement with *God Calling*:

> During that same year I began reading *God Calling*, a devotional book written by two anonymous "listeners." These women practiced waiting quietly in God's Presence, pencils and paper in hand, recording the messages they received from Him. The messages are written in first person, with "I" designating God. While I was living in Japan, someone had mailed this book to me from the U.S.

I had not read it at that time, but I had held onto the book through two international moves. Six or seven years later, this little paperback became *a treasure to me.* It dove-tailed remarkably well with my longing to live in Jesus' Presence.

The following year, I began to wonder if I, too, could receive messages during my times of communing with God. I had been writing in prayer journals for years, but that was one-way communication: I did all the talking. *I knew that God communicated with me through the Bible, but I yearned for more.* Increasingly, I wanted to hear what God had to say to me personally on a given day. I decided to listen to God with pen in hand, *writing down whatever I believed He was saying.*[1] (emphasis added)

For a Christian not to recognize *God Calling* as an occult/New Age book but, rather, to describe it as "a treasure to me" should raise some serious red flags. This brings to mind Jesus' words in Matthew:

For where your treasure is, there will your heart be also. (Matthew 6:21)

It is grievous that, as a longstanding Christian, Sarah Young did not see *God Calling* for what it is—an occult/metaphysical book advocating a number of spiritually dangerous New Age practices and concepts. Now *Jesus Calling* and *God Calling* are bringing meditation, channeling, and spiritual dictation into the Christian church, both with messages similarly arranged as a devotional.

2

CHANNELING JESUS?

Both the "Jesus" of *God Calling* and the "Jesus" of *Jesus Calling* bring the occult/New Age practice of "channeling," or being a "channel," into the church.

CHANNELING HAS LONG been an occult/New Age phenomenon. It is the way that many new and contrary teachings have been introduced to people by a deceptive spirit world. Neale Donald Walsch's *Conversations with God* books were channeled from his "God" and were on the *New York Times* best-seller list for several years. They are filled with "new revelations" and New Age teachings. Shirley MacLaine's pioneering book-based New Age movie *Out on a Limb* that was made for television helped to bring channeling to a mass audience for the first time. Oprah Winfrey has featured channelers on her influential television and radio programs as well. And channelers such as Jane Roberts (channeling Seth), JZ Knight (channeling Ramtha), Esther Hicks (channeling Abraham), Helen Shucman (channeling the "Christ" of *A Course in Miracles*), and

Barbara Marx Hubbard (channeling the "Christ" of *The Revelation* and *The Book of Co-Creation*) have also helped to popularize channeling and occult/New Age teachings. Books like *God Calling* and *Jesus Calling* are playing their part in this process, and the strict barrier between the occult and the church has been gradually beaten down.

In *Jesus Calling*, "Jesus" expressed his desire that people "be a channel" for his presence. The occult meaning of the word "channel" implies being a spiritual conduit for the New Age Christ Energy. Channeling was once an exclusive occult/New Age term. Now it is part of an overlapping vocabulary that is attempting to bring the church

> Christians who interact with the New Age are in danger of being further deceived and may even fall away from their faith.

and the occult world into "unity" and "oneness." The "Jesus" of *Jesus Calling* states:

> I am training you to find Me in each moment and *to be a channel* of My loving Presence.[1] (emphasis added)

> Thus you are doubly blessed, because *a living channel* absorbs some of whatever flows through it.[2] (emphasis added)

> *Be a channel* of My Love, Joy, and Peace by listening to Me as you listen to others.[3] (emphasis added)

If a Christian interacts with the New Age, occult practices are not suddenly legitimized just because they are experienced by Christians. Rather, Christians who interact with the New Age are in danger of being further deceived and may even fall away from their faith. It also needs to be said that Christian efforts to redefine a popular New Age word like "channel" in the attempt to make it Christian causes nothing but confusion and ultimately plays right into our spiritual Adversary's hands. God's people are not called to be channels. They are called to be disciples. Jesus said:

> If ye continue in my word, then are ye my disciples indeed;
> and ye shall know the truth, and the truth shall make you free.
> (John 8:31-32)

3

TEST
THE
SPIRITS

T here is no evidence that the spirits are being tested to see
if Sarah Young's best-selling messages are from the true
Jesus Christ.

GIVEN THAT SARAH Young's "Jesus" is delivering messages
that are being read around the world, it is imperative for readers to
know if she is really hearing from
the true Jesus Christ.

> Beloved, believe not
> every spirit, but try the
> spirits whether they are
> of God: because many
> false prophets are gone
> out into the world

Scripture's warning to
believers to "try the spirits"
(1 John 4:1) is nowhere to be
found in *Jesus Calling*. To the
contrary, when Sarah Young's
"Jesus" is quoted in *Jesus Calling*
as saying, "You must learn to
discern what is My voice and
what is not,"[1] he gives her

some very dangerous counsel. With no mention of 1 Timothy 4:1's warning about "seducing spirits," he says, "Ask My Spirit to give you this discernment."[2] But if the "Jesus" that Sarah Young is listening to is *not* the true Jesus Christ, then this false "Christ" is instructing her to ask *his* spirit to tell her what is true and what is not. Consequently, instead of *testing* the spirit, she is *asking* and *trusting* the spirit that she should be *testing*. This can only lead to greater deception and confusion. This counsel by Sarah Young's "Jesus" cleverly works to prevent the detection of a counterfeit "Jesus," which obviously plays right into the hands of our spiritual Adversary.

> Beloved, believe not every spirit, but try the spirits whether they are of God: because many false prophets are gone out into the world. Hereby know ye the Spirit of God: Every spirit that confesseth that Jesus Christ is come in the flesh is of God: And every spirit that confesseth not that Jesus Christ is come in the flesh is not of God: and this is that spirit of antichrist, whereof ye have heard that it should come; and even now already is it in the world. (1 John 4:1-3)

4

JESUS CONTRADICTS HIMSELF?

I n the Bible, the apostle John wrote the following:

> I have not written unto you because ye know not the truth, but because ye know it, and that *no lie is of the truth.* (1 John 2:21; emphasis added)

ALSO FROM SCRIPTURE we know the true Jesus Christ said:

> I am the way, the truth, and the life: no man cometh unto the Father, but by me. (John 14:6)

Because Jesus Christ *is* the truth, He cannot contradict the truth. But in *Jesus Calling*, this "Jesus" (who claims to be the true Jesus) *does* contradict the truth of the true Jesus Christ. This "Jesus" states:

> I am with you always. These were the last words I spoke before ascending into heaven.[1]

At the end of this day's devotion at the bottom of the page, the reference Matthew 28:20 is given. In Scripture, this verse (which Sarah Young's "Jesus" quotes), records the true Jesus Christ's statement, "lo, I am with you alway," which He spoke after His resurrection. But these were *not* the last words Jesus Christ spoke before ascending into heaven. As author and pastor Larry DeBruyn points out, this "promise of His continued presence" "was to the eleven disciples on a mountain in Galilee (Matthew 28:16, 20)," and His last words "were uttered later on a different mount near Jerusalem" which is the Mount of Olives (Acts 1:12).[2] Immediately prior to ascending into heaven, His *actual* last words were the following—which, as Pastor DeBruyn also points out, "were not that He would be *with* them but rather that they would be His *witnesses*":

> And he said unto them, It is not for you to know the times or the seasons, which the Father hath put in his own power. But ye shall receive power, after that the Holy Ghost is come upon you: and ye shall be witnesses unto me both in Jerusalem, and in all Judaea, and in Samaria, and unto the uttermost part of the earth. *And when he had spoken these things, while they beheld, he was taken up; and a cloud received him out of their sight.* (Acts 1:7-9; emphasis added)

Let's take a look at the very next verses in this passage:

> And while they looked stedfastly toward heaven as he went up, behold, two men stood by them in white apparel; Which also said, Ye men of Galilee, why stand ye gazing up into heaven? *this same Jesus,* which is taken up from you into heaven, *shall so come in like manner as ye have seen him go into heaven.* (Acts 1:10-11; emphasis added)

Is the "Jesus" of *Jesus Calling* this *same* Jesus? No. He cannot possibly be the same, as that "Jesus" openly contradicts what Scripture tells us were Jesus Christ's actual last words before He was taken up, according to Acts 1:7-9. More than ever, we need to heed Jesus' warnings of false Christs and false prophets:

> Then if any man shall say unto you, Lo, here is Christ, or there; believe it not. For there shall arise false Christs, and false prophets, and shall shew great signs and wonders; insomuch that, if it were possible, they shall deceive the very elect. *Behold, I have told you before.* Wherefore if they shall say unto you, Behold, he is in the desert; go not forth: behold, he is in the secret chambers; believe it not. (Matthew 24:23-26; emphasis added)

5

JESUS TELLS US TO LAUGH AT THE FUTURE?

T he "Jesus" of *Jesus Calling* completely contradicts the sober warnings of the true Jesus Christ in Matthew 24, Mark 13, and Luke 21 when he states: "The future is a phantom, seeking to spook you. Laugh at the future!"[1]

IN THE BIBLE, Jesus Christ makes it clear that the future is *no laughing matter*. In Matthew 24 and in other verses, He describes the serious events that will transpire at the end of time as very real and not a phantom. He tells His disciples to "not be troubled" by these future happenings, but He does *not* tell them to take the future lightly or to laugh at the future. Rather, He tells them to watch and be ready and to not be deceived by the false Christs and false prophets that will come in His name (Matthew 24:3-5, 24, 42, 44).

In the book of Revelation, Jesus prophesies of God's impending judgment and about a very real battle of Armageddon (Revelation 16:16). Ecclesiastes 3:4 says there is "a time to weep, and a time to

58

laugh," and the true Jesus makes it very clear that the future is *not* something to laugh at or laugh about. Rather, He warns in Matthew 24 of the increased hatred and persecution toward Christians that will be taking place—that we may even be killed for our faith. It is definitely a time to be taken most seriously. Only a false "Christ" would tell people to laugh at the future.

It is not surprising that the false "Christ" of *A Course in Miracles* promised that "[t]he world will end in laughter."[2] Nor is it surprising that this false "Jesus" of the New Age and the "Jesus" of *God Calling* and of *Jesus Calling* place an unbiblical emphasis on laughter rather than the watchfulness, sobriety, steadfastness, and prayer that is called for in Scripture.

Ecclesiastes 7:3-4 says:

> Sorrow is better than laughter: for by the sadness of the countenance the heart is made better. The heart of the wise is in the house of mourning; but the heart of fools is in the house of mirth.

In Luke 21:19, Jesus Christ does not say "in your laughter possess ye your souls" but, rather, "In your patience possess ye your souls." In regard to the future, the true Jesus Christ tells us to *count the cost* (Luke 14:28), not look for laughs:

> Woe unto you that laugh now! for ye shall mourn and weep. (Luke 6:25)

6

THE FLATTERY OF JESUS?

T he "Jesus" of *Jesus Calling* consistently flatters Sarah Young and her readers. Many of his statements are wholly inconsistent with the way the *true* Jesus related to people as described in the Bible.

JESUS SAID THAT His sheep hear His voice (John 10:3) and they will not follow the voice of a stranger (John 10:5). When looking at these quotes of "Jesus" from *Jesus Calling*, ask yourself—do these statements sound like things our Lord and Savior Jesus Christ would say?

> When you trustingly whisper My Name, My aching ears are soothed.[1]

> When you walk through a day in trusting dependence on Me, My aching heart is soothed.[2]

> As you listen to birds calling to one another, hear also My Love-call to you.[3]

Feel your face tingle as you bask in My Love-Light.[4]

I am aching to hold you in *My everlasting arms,* to enfold you in My Love.[5]

Let My gold-tinged Love wash over you and soak into the depths of your being.[6]

When you seek My Face in response to My Love-call, both of us are blessed.[7]

Look into My Face and feel the warmth of My Love-Light shining upon you.[8]

When your Joy in Me meets My Joy in you, there are fireworks of heavenly ecstasy.[9]

Take time to rest in the Love-Light of My Presence.[10]

The Bible counsels us to:

> Put on the whole armour of God, that ye may be able to stand against the wiles of the devil. (Ephesians 6:11)

And we are warned that "a flattering mouth worketh ruin" (Proverbs 26:28). Unlike the "Jesus" of *Jesus Calling* who does so excessively, Jesus Christ never flattered people. After my days in the New Age movement, I learned how the seductive spirit realm used meditation, channeling, psychic readings, and other occult practices to appeal to our need to feel special or specially cared for. It was seductive flattery, and we fell for it time after time. And it is just this kind of flattery that brought rulers to power and will one day characterize the entry onto the world scene by Antichrist:

> [B]ut he shall come in peaceably, and obtain the kingdom by flatteries. (Daniel 11:21)

7

WHO WANTS US TO REST BY THE WAYSIDE?

C onsider this, why does the "Jesus" of *Jesus Calling* want us to "Take time to rest by the wayside" when Jesus Christ warned that the wayside is where the devil comes to take away the Word of God?

IN *JESUS CALLING*, "Jesus" states: "Take time to rest by the wayside."[1] Likewise, in *God at Eventide: Companion Volume to God Calling* in a section subtitled "Wayside Meetings," "Jesus" states: "Recall our many meetings by the wayside."[2] In the parable of the sower and the seed, the true Jesus Christ *warned* His disciples about the wayside. It was where *the devil* waited to steal the Word of God out of people's hearts (Luke 8:11-12). The wicked one took it from those who heard the Word of God but didn't understand it. The wayside is *anything but* a place to rest.

> Hear ye therefore the parable of the sower. When any one
> heareth the word of the kingdom, and understandeth it not,

62

then cometh the wicked one, and catcheth away that which was sown in his heart. This is he which received seed by the way side. (Matthew 13:18-19)

The "Jesus" of *Jesus Calling* that enticingly calls you to "rest by the wayside" is *not* to be trusted. This is *not* the voice of our Shepherd, the true Jesus Christ.

Given that the wayside is where the devil *takes away* the Word of God, the context of the call of this "Jesus" to leisurely "rest by the wayside" needs to be taken into account. In this day's devotion of *Jesus Calling*, "Jesus" tells us:

Sit quietly in My Presence while I bless you. Make your mind like a still pool of water, ready to *receive* whatever *thoughts* I drop into it. . . .

Take time to rest *by the wayside*, for I am not in a hurry. A leisurely pace accomplishes more than hurried striving.[3] (emphasis added)

With the "Jesus" of *Jesus Calling* waiting to drop "thoughts" into the minds of those by the wayside, also consider the following. The name Legion in Mark 5:9 refers to the name of the unclean spirit that possessed a Gadarene demoniac. When the evil spirit was confronted by Jesus Christ, and Jesus asked the spirit's name, the spirit replied: "My name is Legion: for we are many." The false New Age "Christ" of *A Course in Miracles* states that "Helpers are given you in many forms" and "[t]heir names are legion."[4] And speaking through

> It is demonic spirits—that will "help" guide the minds *stilled by the wayside* into a new way of thinking as the Word of God is taken away.

Barbara Marx Hubbard, the New Age "Christ" also states: "This consciousness is the guide through the transition. It is legion. It manifests by the billions."[5] What is essentially being said here, and in such a cunning way that mockingly plays upon the ignorance of people, is that it is legion—i.e., demonic spirits—that will "help" guide the minds that are *stilled by the wayside* into a *new way of thinking* as the Word of God is taken away. And Scripture tells us that after Legion was sent out of the Gadarene by the true Jesus Christ, people saw him that had been "possessed with the devil, and had the legion, sitting, and clothed, and in his *right mind*: and they were afraid" (Mark 5:15).

8

VISUALIZING JESUS?

Sarah Young engaged in the occult/New Age practice of *creative visualization* when she "pictured" her family "encircled by God's protective presence."

IN THE CHAPTER on visualization of the previously mentioned *Encyclopedia of New Age Beliefs*, Dave Hunt and T.A. McMahon from their book *The Seduction of Christianity* state the following:

> "Visualization" and "guided imagery" have long been recognized by sorcerers of all kinds as the most powerful and effective methodology for contacting the spirit world in order to acquire supernatural power, knowledge, and healing. Such methods are neither taught nor practiced in the Bible as helps to faith or prayer.[1]

Sarah Young wrote that after her two initial spiritual experiences of feeling the presence of "Jesus," she lived "an exemplary Christian life" for the next sixteen years.[2] During this time, there was no further contact with the presence. Then after moving to Australia and while doing ministry there with her husband, she experienced the presence once again after she "visualized God":

> One morning as I prayed, *I visualized God* protecting each of us. I pictured first our daughter, then our son, and then Steve encircled by God's protective Presence, which looked like golden light. When I prayed for myself, I was suddenly enveloped in brilliant light and profound peace. I lost all sense of time as I experienced God's Presence in this powerful way.[3] (emphasis added)

However, Sarah Young had unwittingly engaged in the occult/New Age practice of *creative visualization.* Believers can obviously pray and ask for God's protection, but we are *not* to try and orchestrate that protection through our own imaginative powers. God will not be manipulated, either by us or by our techniques—and especially if they are of the occult. Rather, engaging in occult practices, even innocently, can open a door into the deceptive spirit world (Ephesians 4:27; 1 Timothy 4:1). And Christians who naively open an occult door by using the practice of creative visualization are not immune to being deceived.

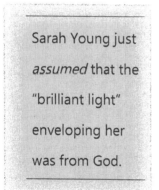

Sarah Young just *assumed* that the "brilliant light" enveloping her was from God.

Sarah Young just *assumed* that the "brilliant light" enveloping her was from God. But one cannot just assume anything—especially after engaging in an occult practice as she did. It wouldn't be surprising if the demonic spirit realm was giving her the kind of experience that she was yearning for. The spirit world is only too glad to jump at the chance of deceiving someone—especially those who use occult/New Age practices.

Some of us have learned the hard way that Satan and his deceptive spirits can come as angels of light. I was initially seduced into the New Age when a ball of light suddenly appeared over my head during a psychic reading. The psychic told me the ball of light was a sign that I had "a lot of help on the other side."[4]

> There is good reason why Scripture warns that Satan "is transformed into an angel of light" and his ministers "as the ministers of righteousness."

There is good reason why Scripture warns that Satan "is transformed into an angel of light" and his ministers "as the ministers of righteousness" (2 Corinthians 11:14-15). And this is why we are told to "try the spirits" to know if they are of God (1 John 4:1). Eventually, I would discover how deceived I had been by the ball of light, as well as by the New Age "Jesus" I had been following in *A Course in Miracles* and in other false teachings. Jesus warned:

> Take heed therefore that the light which is in thee be not darkness. (Luke 11:35)

When I accepted Jesus as my Savior, I not only stopped meditation, contemplative prayer, creative visualization, and all my other occult practices, I asked the Lord to forgive me for ever getting involved with them in the first place. No matter how right they may seem and feel, occult/New Age practices are still "heathen" practices. Scripture tells us:

> Thus saith the LORD, Learn not the way of the heathen. (Jeremiah 10:2)

Many New Age books advocate creative visualization—a practice which provides a perfect opportunity for the spirit world to bring deception. *Creative Visualization* is the title of a best-selling book that is authored by Shakti Gawain. Ophiel is another occult author and practitioner who has written *The Art and Practice of Getting Material Things Through Creative Visualization*. Ophiel dedicated this book as follows:

> OPHIEL dedicates this book to all those who are endeavoring to better themselves, mentally, physically, and materially thru the study, practice, and application of THE OCCULT.[5]

And in the section of Ophiel's book called, "The Art and Practice of Creative Visualization," he describes the occult underpinnings of creative visualization:

> CREATIVE VISUALIZATION is the name for a Magical-Occult-Operation wherein a man creates in his "Mind's eye," or in his imagination, the idea-image of something, or some circumstance, or some circumstances he fancies.[6]

> There is a way which seemeth right unto a man, but the end thereof are the ways of death. (Proverbs 14:12)

9

THE DARK NIGHT OF JESUS' BIRTH?

In *Jesus Calling*, "Jesus" states that he was born in a "filthy stable" "under the most appalling conditions." He says that the night of his birth was a "dark night" for him.

IN WHAT CAN only be described as the ultimate revisionist description of the night of Jesus' birth, Sarah Young's "Jesus" openly bemoans what he describes as that "dark night for Me." He states in *Jesus Calling*:

> Try to imagine what I gave up when I came into your world as a baby. I set aside My Glory, so that I could identify with mankind. *I accepted the limitations of infancy under the most appalling conditions—a filthy stable. That was a dark night for Me*, even though angels lit up the sky proclaiming "Glory!" to awe-struck shepherds.[1] (emphasis added)

This doesn't sound like the voice of *our Savior*—it sounds instead like the voice of *a stranger* (John 10:5). And when you really think about it, wouldn't it be more likely that Satan himself would be the one to describe the night of Jesus' birth as that "dark night for me"?

As to the bemoaning of this "Jesus," Scripture tells us to be content in whatever circumstances we find ourselves:

> Not that I speak in respect of want: for I have learned, in whatsoever state I am, therewith to be content. (Philippians 4:11)

In whatever way this devotion in *Jesus Calling* is looked at, it is a very unbiblical message. The conditions of His birth were not "*appalling*" but, rather, God's "*sign*" to the shepherds, and then they, after seeing "the babe lying in a manger," *glorified* and *praised God* for "*all*" they had "*seen*":

> For unto you is born this day in the city of David a Saviour, which is Christ the Lord. And this shall be *a sign unto you; Ye shall find the babe wrapped in swaddling clothes, lying in a manger*. . . . And it came to pass, as the angels were gone away from them into heaven, the shepherds said one to another, Let us now go even unto Bethlehem, and see this thing which is come to pass, which the Lord hath made known unto us. And they came with haste, and found Mary, and Joseph, and the babe lying in a manger. . . . And the shepherds returned, *glorifying and praising God for all the things that they had heard and seen,* as it was told unto them. (Luke 2:11-20) (emphasis added)

10

ABRAHAM GUILTY OF "IDOLATRY" & "SON-WORSHIP"?

The "Jesus" of *Jesus Calling* states that Abraham, in regard to his son Isaac, was guilty of "son-worship," "undisciplined emotions," and "idolatry." This is not biblical.

IN *JESUS CALLING*, "Jesus" states:

> Remember the extreme measures I used with Abraham and Isaac. I took Isaac to the very point of death to free Abraham from son-worship. Both Abraham and Isaac suffered terribly because of the father's undisciplined emotions. I detest idolatry, even in the form of parental love.[1]

This account by the "Jesus" of *Jesus Calling* is as bizarre as it is unbiblical. Abraham, with whom God made His covenant, was not guilty of worshiping his son Isaac, and he was not idolatrous. To the contrary, he exhibited the utmost faith and obedience to God both in his life and in his actions. Hebrews 11:17 records:

> By faith Abraham, when he was tried, offered up Isaac: and he that had received the promises offered up his only begotten son.

Abraham simply proved his willingness to do God's will—whatever the cost.

> By myself have I sworn, saith the LORD, for because thou hast done this thing, and hast not withheld thy son, thine only son: That in blessing I will bless thee . . . And in thy seed shall all the nations of the earth be blessed; because thou hast obeyed my voice. (Genesis 22:16-18)

It is quite telling that the first time the word *worship* appears in God's Word, it is in regard to this willingness of Abraham to obey God by offering up his only son:

> Both Abraham and Isaac suffered terribly because of the father's undisciplined emotions. I detest idolatry, even in the form of parental love.—Sarah Young's "Jesus"

And Abraham said unto his young men, Abide ye here with the ass; and I and the lad will go yonder and *worship*, and come again to you. And Abraham took the wood of the burnt offering, and laid it upon Isaac his son; and he took the fire in his hand, and a knife; and they went both of them together. . . . And they came to the place which God had told him of; and Abraham built an altar there, and laid the wood in order, and bound Isaac his son, and laid him on the altar upon the wood. And Abraham stretched forth his hand, and took the knife to slay his son. (Genesis 22:5-6, 9-10; emphasis added)

Matthew Henry's lengthy commentary about this event, is filled with praise for Abraham's character, faithfulness, and obedience. Henry wrote:

> Be astonished, O heavens! at this; and wonder, O earth! Here is an act of faith and obedience, which deserves to be a spectacle to God, angels, and men.[2]

Abraham's willingness to sacrifice his own son followed by God's intervention with a substitute sacrifice both foreshadow God's willingness to offer His only begotten son as a substitute offering for the sins of the world. Are we to suddenly believe that this was a disciplinary measure rather than God's demonstration of Abraham's faith in God? No, this had nothing to do with "son-worship," "undisciplined emotions," or "idolatry." This was the ultimate worship and love for God. This perversion of Scripture by the "Jesus" of *Jesus Calling* can entice the undiscerning reader into believing this extra-biblical account, which attempts to provide *new revelations.*

It is not insignificant that this "other Jesus" speaks in condemning tones about Abraham while the real Jesus spoke favorably of Abraham, saying of him: who "rejoiced to see my day: and he saw it, and was glad" (John 8:56). Abraham is the one chosen for God's covenant with man—which was confirmed in the true Jesus Christ (Galatians 3:15-18). And Abraham is the one chosen for God's foreshadowing of the sacrifice of His Son—the true sinless Jesus Christ Who died for our sins (1 John 3:5). And it is Abraham's seed that is the seed chosen for God's children—as Scripture says, every believer becomes Abraham's seed when they put their faith in the true Jesus Christ:

> For ye are all the children of God by faith in Christ Jesus. . . . And if ye be Christ's, then are ye Abraham's seed, and heirs according to the promise. (Galatians 3:26, 29)

> Know ye therefore that they which are of faith, the same
> are the children of Abraham. . . . So then they which be of
> faith are blessed with faithful Abraham. (Galatians 3:7, 9)

No, it is not insignificant that "faithful Abraham" is the one chosen for the condemning tones of the "Jesus" in *Jesus Calling*. Abraham, like all of us, was not sinless, but Sarah Young's "Jesus" has sorely misconstrued him.

The lesson here is the sufficiency of God's inspired Holy Bible and a warning to those who would seek to add to it or subtract from it and pervert what God has inspired.

> All scripture is given by inspiration of God. (2 Timothy 3:16)

> Add thou not unto his words, lest he reprove thee, and thou
> be found a liar. (Proverbs 30:6)

11

Contemplative Prayer, the New Age, & Psalm 46:10

C ountless references to meditating, being quiet, being still, relaxing, resting, letting go, and reciting Psalm 46:10 are found throughout *God Calling* and *Jesus Calling*. They are all suggested ways of entering into *the silence* to experience God's presence.

THE NEW AGE/New Spirituality likewise places great emphasis on these same ways of entering the silence in order to experience God's presence.

The reason so much emphasis has been put on stillness and invoking Psalm 46:10 in the New Age/New Spirituality is because stillness has provided a "channel" for supernatural communication. What I came to realize years ago was that the silence allowed deceptive spirits to establish contact with those of us who were naive and undiscerning "listeners." The conditions of stillness, openness, and receptivity were ideal for deceptive spirits to inject ungodly thoughts and understandings into our minds. And now the same thing is going on in the church which sees no need to test the spirits. Along with testing the spirits, Scripture also warns us:

> Wherefore gird up the loins of your mind, be sober, and hope to the end for the grace that is to be brought unto you at the revelation of Jesus Christ. (1 Peter 1:13)

There is good reason why the "Jesus" of *Jesus Calling* wants those he calls to "Come to Me with your defenses down" and "Relax"[1]:

> Make your mind like a still pool of water, *ready to receive whatever thoughts I drop into it.*[2] (emphasis added)

> Sit quietly in My Presence, *letting My thoughts reprogram your thinking.*[3] (emphasis added)

> *Let Me control your mind.*[4] (emphasis added)

The "Jesus" of *God Calling* says:

> Remember that I can work through you better when you are at rest.[5]

Similarly, the "Jesus" of *Jesus Calling* says:

> I can do My best handiwork when you sit in the stillness of My Presence, focusing your entire being on Me.[6]

The "Jesus" of *God Calling* urges readers to "cultivate silence":

> *Cultivate silence.* "God speaks in silences." A silence, a soft wind. Each can be a message to convey My meaning to the heart.[7] (emphasis added)

And, in like manner, New Age matriarch Alice Bailey's channeled spirit guide Djwhal Khul said:

> One of the primary conditions that a disciple has to *cultivate*, in order to sense the plan and be used by the Master, is *solitude*.[8] (emphasis added)

There is nothing in Scripture that tells us to let our "defenses down" and sit in silence. Scripture tells us instead:

> Casting down imaginations, and every high thing that exalteth itself against the knowledge of God, and bringing into captivity every thought to the obedience of Christ. (2 Corinthians 10:5)

It is a simple fact that many of the teachings and communications we received in the New Age were channeled during meditative and contemplative quiet times when we were absorbed in the silence. In our New Age meditations, we would sometimes meditate on and contemplate certain passages of Scripture. At an Edgar Cayce conference I once attended, we began each day by meditating on Psalm 46:10—"Be still, and know that I am God." Looking back on that experience now, I understand why that particular Psalm was used by so many New Age groups for contemplation and meditation. The spirit world was only too willing to take something the true God was saying about *Himself* and translate it into something the occult/New Age was saying about *man*. It was a very clever tactic.

> Many of the teachings and communications we received in the New Age were channeled during meditative and contemplative quiet times when we were absorbed in the silence.

We were being "still" and we were quoting Scripture, but we were continually affirming that *we* were God by emphasizing the "I" as we repeated the phrase *I am God* over and over again. We were "going within" to the "god within." *Be still* and know that "I" am *God*. In our open and unguarded state of "being still" we were not being taught that God was God. We were being taught that "*we*" were God.

The "Jesus" of *A Course in Miracles* also used Psalm 46:10 to deceptively teach this New Age concept. We were to "be still" and to *know* that *we* were God. This false "Jesus" actually used this verse to introduce his heretical teaching that "[t]he journey to the cross should be the last 'useless journey.'"[9] Our New Age journey was *around* the Cross, not *through* the Cross. We learned from *A Course in Miracles* and our other New Age teachings that we didn't need Jesus Christ as our Lord and Savior. Rather, we could save ourselves by "being still" and "awakening" to the inner self-realization that *we* were God.

EILEEN CADDY AND FINDHORN

IRONICALLY, Psalm 46:10 was the founding credo of the pioneering New Age community of Findhorn in Scotland. Co-founder Eileen Caddy distinctly heard the words "Be still and know that I am God" in a meditation, and as a result Findhorn was founded on this Bible verse. She described her "Be still" experience:

> Yes, we were like children then, and God was still somewhat like the Father, separate and above us, reaching down to help. But gradually I have come to understand what it means to find that same God within myself. . . .

> The first time I heard this voice was in 1953, when Peter and I were visiting Glastonbury, a center of spiritual power in England. I was sitting in the stillness of a small private sanctuary there, when I heard a voice—a very clear voice—within me. I had never experienced anything like that before. It simply said, *Be still and know that I am God*. What is this?

I thought. Am I going mad? I had been brought up in the Church of England and learned in Sunday school about the "still small voice within"—but when you actually *hear* a voice, it's a different matter. I was really quite shocked, because it was so clear.[10]

"God" later told her:

What greater or more wonderful relationship could man ask for than the knowledge that he is truly one with Me, and that *I am in you and you are in Me*.[11] (emphasis added)

She wrote:

Accepting the reality of this oneness came slowly. In fact, at first I felt it was audacious even to speak of such a thing. *Yet I couldn't deny my experience.* I know that God is within each one of us, within everything. I feel that the Church teaches about the God outside of us, but that's the same God as the one within. You can call him by different names if you like, but there's only one God.[12] (emphasis added)

MISUSE OF PSALM 46:10

EILEEN Caddy's New Age understanding of the "God within" and "oneness" started with an inner voice that told her "Be still and know that I am God." Like Caddy, so many people who have been raised in today's church have been similarly deceived into believing that the "be still" verse from Psalm 46:10 is God's heavenly instruction to enter into solitude and silence so they can hear His voice. Ironically, the real meaning of this verse has *nothing* to do with sitting in silence, practicing the presence, or any meditative practice. Undiscerning church leaders have misappropriated Psalm 46:10 to justify contemplative prayer. They now use this verse to incubate a "conversation with God."

Trusted Bible commentaries and discerning pastors teach that the command in Psalm 46:10—"Be still, and know that I am God: I will be exalted among the heathen, I will be exalted in the earth"—is a call to faith and obedience, not to contemplative prayer. Matthew Henry's respected Bible commentary presents a more accurate exposition of this verse:

> Let his enemies be still, and threaten no more, but know it, to their terror, that he is God, one infinitely above them . . . he will be exalted among the heathen and not merely among his own people, he will be exalted in the earth and not merely in the church. . . . Let his own people be still; let them be calm and sedate, and tremble no more, but know, to their comfort, that the Lord is God, he is God alone, and will be exalted above the heathen.[13]

Using Psalm 46:10 as a call to practice contemplative prayer is completely contrary to the intent of this passage of Scripture. However, this is what is being advocated in the New Age/New Spirituality, the emerging church, *God Calling*, and *Jesus Calling*. In fact, the "Jesus" of *Jesus Calling* falsely teaches that Psalm 46:10 was given as a command to "sit quietly" in his presence:

> The world has changed enormously since I first gave the command to *be still and know that I am God*. However, this timeless truth is essential for the well-being of your soul. As dew refreshes grass and flowers during the stillness of the night, so My Presence revitalizes you as you sit quietly with Me.[14]

Sarah Young also states in her "Introduction" to *Jesus Calling*:

> A life-changing verse has been "Be still, and know that I
> am God" (Psalm 46:10). Alternate readings for "Be still"
> are "Relax," "Let go," and "Cease striving" (NASB). This
> is an enticing invitation from God to lay down our cares
> and seek His Presence. I believe that God yearns for these
> quiet moments with us even more than we do. . . .
>
> This practice of listening to God has increased my intimacy
> with Him more than any other spiritual discipline, so I
> want to share some of the messages I have received.[15]

This "enticing invitation" does *not* come from God. Her
interpretation misses the real meaning of the verse and is actually
more consistent with the New Age *twisting* of this verse. God
definitely meets us in our prayer times as well as when we think on
Scripture, but Psalm 46:10 is *not* an invitation to be still and listen
for God's voice. Rather, God is calling Israel into an attitude of quiet
faith and rest in which His people will trust that no matter how
perilous the times, He is working out His plan among the nations.
Everybody is to literally *be still, know He is God*, and know that *He
will be exalted* among the nations and in the earth.

Sarah Young followed up her erroneous teaching on Psalm
46:10 by stating that "God yearns for these quiet moments with us
even more than we do." This is reminiscent of the "I need you more
than you need Me"[16] statement that was uttered by the "Jesus" in
God Calling. Nothing in Scripture substantiates either one of these
statements. And there is nothing in Scripture about being still and
sitting with pen in hand waiting to hear a message from God while
practicing the presence and doing contemplative prayer.

BIBLICAL MEDITATION

BIBLICAL meditation is different. We are to meditate on—think
on—His Word, His precepts, His laws, His attributes, His statutes,
His testimonies, and His works.

Mine eyes prevent the night watches, that I might meditate in thy word. (Psalm 119:148)

But his delight is in the law of the LORD; and in his law doth he meditate day and night. (Psalm 1:2)

I have more understanding than all my teachers: for thy testimonies are my meditation. (Psalm 119:99)

I remember the days of old; I meditate on all thy works; I muse on the work of thy hands. (Psalm 143:5)

If whispers repeat the Word of God, then they are unnecessary.

If whispers contradict the Word of God, then they are heresy.

If they add to the Word of God, then they point to Scripture's

inadequacy and insufficiency. To this point Proverbs warns:

"Add thou not unto his [God's] words, lest he [God] reprove

thee, and thou be found a liar"*[17]* (Proverbs 30:6).

—Pastor Larry DeBruyn

12

Practicing What Presence?

T he word "Presence" is found more than 365 times in *Jesus Calling*. The term is also commonly used in the New Age/ New Spirituality.

NEW AGE MATRIARCH Alice Bailey, New Age leader Barbara Marx Hubbard, and countless other New Age/New Spirituality figures have used the term *presence* to refer to the "God" and "Christ" of the New Age movement. Metaphysician Joel Goldsmith wrote a best-selling book titled *Practicing the Presence* that many of us used in the New Age. Here are a few quotes from his book regarding "God" and "presence" in his New Age teachings. The quotes highlight the growing indistinguishability of the use of the word *presence* in both New Age books and reputed "Christian" books like *God Calling* and *Jesus Calling*. Goldsmith wrote:

> *All is God manifested.* God alone constitutes this universe; *God constitutes the life, the mind, and the Soul of every individual.*[1] (emphasis added)

Through study and meditation, eventually we shall come to *that God-contact within us,* wherein we receive the divine assurance, "Lo, I am with you always," the continuous assurance of *the one Presence,* one Power, one Being, one Life, one Law in which there are no evil powers or destructive forces. It is in this awareness of *oneness* that we find our peace.[2] (emphasis added)

We, who are *practicing the Presence,* are of the few who know what ultimately will save the world. . . . We need only withdraw into ourselves and contemplate *our oneness with God and with one another.*[3] (emphasis added)

Hundreds of books have been written on this subject, but those that have been written out of the depths of experience all agree that *the presence of God* can only be realized when *the senses are stilled,* when we have settled down into an atmosphere of expectancy, of hope, and of faith. In this *state of relaxation* and peace, we wait. That is all we can do, just wait. We cannot bring God to us for God is already here, in this *inner stillness,* in this quietness and confidence.[4] (emphasis added)

SARAH YOUNG AND BARBARA MARX HUBBARD

IN *Volume 2* of her book *"Reimagining" God,* the late Christian author Tamara Hartzell points out the similarity between Sarah Young and New Age leader Barbara Marx Hubbard, both with pen in hand, experiencing the "presence" of "Christ":

In *Jesus Calling,* Young writes of becoming "aware of *a lovely Presence*" . . . an "encounter with the Presence of Jesus." She writes: "I knew that God communicated with me through the Bible, but I yearned for more." So "*with pen in hand*" she began a *"new way of communicating with God"* and writes that "I have continued to receive personal messages from God as I *meditate* on Him." Young also writes that her *"journaling"* "changed from monologue to dialogue" and the "messages began to flow more freely." She also writes:

"This practice of listening to God has increased my intimacy with Him more than any other *spiritual discipline*, so I want to share *some of the messages I have received.* . . . I have written them *from Jesus' point of view*: i.e. . . . . (*I, Me, Mine*) *always refer to Christ*."

This is all quite reminiscent of Barbara Marx Hubbard who likewise writes in *The Revelation* that she "felt a presence"—a "presence" that "continued to communicate an inner stream of ideas" which she wrote in her *"journal."* Along with writing that "[t]he presence was the Christ," Hubbard even writes that "the presence I had experienced was Jesus Christ," and she also refers to it as "the Christ presence" and "the Presence." And in *Birth 2012 and Beyond*, Hubbard writes that her "practice for many years has been to sit in silence, to do a meditation, and then to feel the impulse of creativity coming up . . ." And this includes in "journal writing" in which she "allow[s] the inner voice to write." Hubbard also writes that in the "safe inner space" of *"silence and solitude,"* and the "Inner Sanctuary" of "meditation," "the wise and beloved inner voice" became her "guidance" and "agent of transformation."[5]

The question that must be asked is why are there so few warnings about the role of seducing spirits in this whole meditation-contemplative prayer-practicing the presence process? They are called seducing spirits for a reason, and the church today is comprised of many people who have been seduced in this way. They are spending more and more of their time "soaking" in the presence of an unholy spirit and less and less time reading and understanding the Word of God.

Sarah Young's "Jesus" in *Jesus Calling* presumes that his presence is to be sought "above all else,"[6] which is "My universal Presence."[7] And this same "Jesus" in Sarah Young's 2012 book, *Jesus Today*, counsels the following as well:

> So don't neglect the discipline of practicing My Presence.[8]

BROTHER LAWRENCE AND
PRACTICING THE PRESENCE

PRACTICING the presence was introduced through the published writings of a French Catholic Carmelite monk named Brother Lawrence who lived in the latter half of the 17th century. His book *The Practice of the Presence of God* has been extremely popular through the years. Practicing the presence was first introduced as an interpretation of Isaiah 26:3—"Thou wilt keep him in perfect peace whose mind is stayed on Thee." However, most people don't realize that Brother Lawrence *and* the Catholic Church today are both linked to the foundational New Age/New Spirituality teaching that God is "in" everyone.

The 1994 *Catechism of the Catholic Church*, which is the official source for all Roman Catholic doctrine today, states:

> Let us rejoice then and give thanks that we have become not only Christians, but Christ himself. Do you understand and grasp, brethren, God's grace toward us? Marvel and rejoice: we have become Christ. (#795)[9]

> "For the Son of God became man so that we might become God." (#460)[10]

"The only-begotten Son of God, wanting to make us sharers in his divinity, assumed our nature, so that he, made man, might make men gods." (#460)[11]

When I ordered Brother Lawrence's book *The Practice of the Presence of God* from Amazon.com, the book that arrived included some of his additional writings. This book of collected writings is titled *The Practice of the Presence of God with Spiritual Maxims*. And in the "Spiritual Maxims," under the heading "Of Necessary Practices For Attaining To The Spiritual Life," Brother Lawrence introduced the occult/New Age teaching that God is "in" everyone—"at the very depth and centre of your soul." He said:

> When we are busied, or meditating on spiritual things, even in our time of set devotion, whilst our voice is rising in prayer, we ought to cease for one brief moment, as often as we can, to worship God *in the depth of our being*, to taste Him though it be in passing, to touch Him as it were by stealth. Since you cannot but know that God is with you in all you undertake, that He is at the very depth and centre of your soul.[12]

> These our acts of worship are to be prompted and guided by *faith*. We must unfeignedly believe that God is in very fact within our souls, and that we must worship Him and love Him and serve Him in spirit and in truth.[13]

This is almost exactly what the "Jesus" of *God Calling* told the Two Listeners:

> Wherever the soul is, I am. Man has rarely understood this. I *am* actually at the centre of every man's being, but, distracted with the things of the sense-life, he finds Me not.[14]

And it is almost exactly what metaphysical/New Age author Joel Goldsmith taught in his book *Practicing the Presence:*

> All is God manifested. God alone constitutes this universe; *God constitutes* the life, the mind, and *the Soul* of *every* individual.[15] (emphasis added)

As previously addressed in Section 4 of Part One, God does not naturally and universally reside "in" every person. God is not in the soul or at the center of every man's being. Believers need to adhere to Scripture so they do not become involved with spiritual practices dangerously interwoven with New Age teachings. Faith comes from hearing the Word of God, not from spiritual experience.

> So then faith cometh by hearing, and hearing by the Word of God. (Romans 10:17)

> To the law and to the testimony: if they speak not according to this word, it is because there is no light in them. (Isaiah 8:20)

13

"CO-CREATING" WITH GOD

In *Jesus Calling*, "Jesus" mentions a key New Age term: *co-creation*. Many people do not realize that co-creation is a New Age evolutionary concept that teaches that man *as* God co-creates *with* God because man *is* God also. But man is *not* God.

CO-CREATION IS A New Age concept that entails the necessity of man recognizing that he *is* God and then acting *as* God to *co-create* a positive future. The means to accomplishing this has been laid out by the New Age "Christ" in top New Age leader Barbara Marx Hubbard's book *The Revelation*—which essentially rewrites the Holy Bible's book of Revelation. The New Age "Christ" has a plan and is promising the world that Armageddon is avoidable and that world peace is possible *if* everyone collaborates and *co-creates* with him. He and humanity together can thus save the world. Speaking through Hubbard in *The Revelation*, the New Age "Christ" uses the terms *co-create, co-creation, co-creative, co-creator*, and *co-creatorship* over 100 times. Co-creation is the key to his counterfeit plan of salvation for planet Earth.

Webster's New World Dictionary's sole definition of a *collabora-tionist* is "a person who cooperates with an enemy invader."[1] And the "Jesus" of *Jesus Calling* uses the terms *collaborate, collaborating*, or *collaboration* at least ten times. For example, he states:

> This is a very practical way of *collaborating* with Me. I, the Creator of the universe, have deigned to *co-create* with you.[2] (emphasis added)

In *Jesus Calling*, "Jesus" plays into this ultimate New Age collaboration when he talks of humanity *collaborating* and *co-creating* with him. Again, co-creation is the key to the spirit world's counterfeit plan of salvation for planet Earth. Occult/New Age author Neale Donald Walsch has been taking spiritual dictation from his New Age "God" for many years now. "God"—speaking through Walsch—has proclaimed that "The era of the Single Savior" is to be replaced with "co-creation":

> Yet let me make something clear. *The era of the Single Savior is over.* What is needed now is joint action, combined effort, collective *co-creation*.[3] (emphasis added)

And Hubbard's New Age "Christ" states:

> Here we are, now poised either on the brink of destruction greater than the world has ever seen—a destruction which will cripple planet Earth forever and release only the few to go on—or on the threshold of *global co-creation* wherein each person on Earth will be attracted to participate in his or her own evolution to godliness.[4] (emphasis added)

In *"Reimagining" God,* Tamara Hartzell underscores the connection between co-creation, meditation, and contemplative prayer by quoting the following from Hubbard's book *The Revelation*:

We too *shall* all be changed. . . . the next stage of evolution, the shift from creature to co-creative human. . . .

We draw from all great avatars and paths, but we know that our challenge is to *be* the co-creative human ourselves. There is no outside person or power that can do this for us. Each of us chooses the disciplines and practices that are most compatible with our temperament. We become faithful to those practices, whether they be meditation, yoga, prayer, contemplation—whatever inner work *works*, we do faithfully.[5]

Hartzell also points out the striking similarities of the dictated messages given to both Young and Hubbard by their Presence:

[I]n *Jesus Calling*, Young's "Presence" of "Jesus" that wants to "reprogram your thinking" looks for "an *awakened* soul" in order "to *co-create* with you." Young's "Presence" that also says, "I am all around you, like a *cocoon of Light*," wants you to "[l]earn to tune in to My living Presence by seeking Me in silence," "[a]ttune yourself to My voice," and "do not relinquish your attentiveness to Me." Likewise, in *The Revelation*, Hubbard's "Christ presence" that refers to "humanity *awakening*" as "*co-creators* with Christ" wants you to: "Create the *cocoon of light*. Materialize *my body of light* in your mind's eye." And also: "Keep your attention on me at all times. Practice continually tuning in."[6]

Speaking through Hubbard in *The Revelation,* the New Age "Christ" states:

At the moment of cosmic contact, I will appear to you both through inner experience and through external communication in your mass media—the nervous system of the world.

> You will all feel, hear, and see *my presence* at *one instant in time*, each in your own way.[7] (emphasis added)

This New Age "Christ" further elaborates on this *co-creative* process by describing the moment of experiencing his *presence* as the *Quantum Instant*. He also describes the judgment that will come with it, which will be based on people's willingness to *co-create* the future with him. He states:

> At the time of the *Quantum Instant* there will be a judgment of the quick and the dead. That is, there will be an evolutionary selection process based on your qualifications for *co-creative power*.[8] (emphasis added)

> Those of you who happen to be alive at the time of the actual *Quantum Instant,* will be changed while still alive. . . .

> Your *co-creative system* will turn on. It is being prepared now.[9] (emphasis added)

There is a definite overlap of terms as the "Jesus" of *Jesus Calling* uses this same *co-creative* term to describe how he will transform people's lives. And Hartzell explains why both Sarah Young's "Christ" and Barbara Marx Hubbard's "Christ" contradict Scripture when they talk of man *co-creating* with God:

> It is Jesus Christ of Nazareth—and He alone is Christ— that is one with God. Jesus said, "I and my Father are one" (John 10:30). And it is Jesus Christ of Nazareth, Who alone is Christ, that is the Father's ("co-") Creator. God's Word also tells us: "God, who created all things by Jesus Christ" (Ephesians 3:9). Man is neither one with God nor God's "co-creator." Man never has been and never will be a "natural Christ."[10]

14

QUANTUM LEAP, QUANTUM "CHRIST"

Quantum leap is another term with significant New Age meaning. Although *quantum leap* is a term derived from quantum physics, New Age leaders use quantum physics in their attempt to scientifically prove that God is "in" everything. And the "Jesus" of *Jesus Calling* states:

> When you make that *quantum leap* into eternity, you will find Me awaiting you in heaven.[1]

THE TERM *QUANTUM* leap has been used by New Age proponents to describe the *paradigm shift* that will take place when humanity *awakens* and *evolves* by accepting the New Age/New Worldview that we are all "one" because God is "in" everyone and everything.

In Barbara Marx Hubbard's *The Revelation*, the New Age "Christ" states the following in regard to *co-creating* the conditions to bring forth the *Quantum Instant* and the *Quantum Transformation* that take place with that final *quantum leap*:

A Quantum Transformation is the time of selection of what evolves from what devolves. The species known as *self-centered humanity* will become extinct. The species known as whole-centered humanity [those who believe that God is "in" everyone] will evolve.² (emphasis added)

After the selection process, you will be born to the next stage of evolution. There will be a *New Heaven,* a New Earth, a new body and a new consciousness for all who survive.

The *New Heaven* is you as a *natural Christ,* beginning your life in the universal community.³ (emphasis added)

> The New Age "Christ" is saying, in effect—Those of you who believe God is "in" everyone will make that quantum leap.

The New Age "Christ" is saying, in effect—Those of you who believe God is "in" everyone will make that *quantum leap* at the *Quantum Instant* during the *Quantum Transformation* and will find me—the "Christ" of the New Age (Antichrist)—awaiting you in the New Heaven (counterfeit). Those of you who are *self-centered*—who don't believe that God is "in" everyone and refuse to make that *quantum leap* by believing in humanity's divinity—will not survive *my* judgment (by Antichrist). Regarding the New Age "Christ's" plan and this whole Quantum phenomenon, Hubbard states:

> At the very horizon of our vision we see the resurrected Christ drawing us forward to radically transform. We shall have life everlasting as transformed persons in transformed bodies in a transformed world. When science of mind (spiritual wisdom and practice) and science of matter (the ability to co-evolve with nature) are joined for the purpose of the evolution of the

human race, *we take the quantum leap.* The former things will indeed be passed away.[4] (emphasis added)

Given all of the New Age implications of the false Christ, it is inconceivable that the true Jesus Christ would ever use a term like "quantum leap." But the "Jesus" of *Jesus Calling* states:

When you make that *quantum leap* into eternity, you will find Me awaiting you in heaven.[5]

It is important to note that this statement is consistent with the "Quantum Instant" and the "Quantum Transformation" plans of the New Age "Christ."

In William Paul Young's book, *The Shack*, "God" introduces quantum physics by referring to the "quantum stuff" that is at the "subatomic level"[6] while "Jesus" nonchalantly proclaims that God is "in" everything.[7] In *Jesus Calling*, "Jesus" seems to be on the same "subatomic" track when his use of the term "quantum leap" is followed up later by referring to "mysteries" that are "submerged beneath the surface of the visible world":

Submerged beneath the surface of the visible world are mysteries too vast for you to comprehend.[8]

And who will ultimately explain these esoteric mysteries to us? Perhaps Sarah Young's "Jesus"—if you keep reading her books and practicing the presence of her "Jesus" who states:

I will lead you along *fresh trails* of adventure, *revealing to you things you did not know.* Stay in communication with Me. Follow My guiding Presence.[9] (emphasis added)

It is entirely possible that the role this "Jesus" will play in the future will be "revealing to you things" such as quantum physics seeming to scientifically prove the "mystery" that God is "in" everything. In my book *A "Wonderful" Deception*, I describe how Pastor Annette Capps has a best-selling publication titled *Quantum Faith*. In it, she recommends a New Age book on quantum physics and includes a very telling remark by her father, Pastor Charles Capps. She writes:

> As I studied the theories of quantum physics, I was reminded of a prophecy given by my father, author and teacher Charles Capps, "Some things which have required faith to believe will no longer require faith, for it will be proven to be scientific fact."[10]

The Bible speaks to all those in the New Age and the church who are being deceived by the spiritual misuse of science:

> O Timothy, keep that which is committed to thy trust, avoiding profane and vain babblings, and oppositions of science falsely so called: Which some professing have erred concerning the faith. (1 Timothy 6:20-21)

Will faith in God's Word become a thing of the past as "science" replaces faith? A growing number of church figures have directly or indirectly introduced quantum physics with its New Age implications into their teachings and writings. And all things indicate that God "in" everyone and everything will be the *quantum lie* that will prompt a massively deceived world to take that ultimate quantum leap into a universal, co-created New Age/New Spirituality/New Worldview that will unite them with the Antichrist in his earthly and satanic "New Heaven." And in a statement that New Age leaders couldn't say any better, "Jesus" already says most explicitly in *Jesus Calling*:

> When you seek My Face, put aside thoughts of everything else. *I am above all, as well as in all.*[11] (emphasis added)

15

"COCOON OF LIGHT"

The "Christ" of the New Age refers to the birth of a new humanity awakening to the understanding that we are all "One" because we are all "God." Humanity is described as an emerging butterfly still at the chrysalis or "cocoon" stage that is preparing to *emerge* into "Oneness" from its caterpillar stage to that of a butterfly.

SPEAKING FOR THE New Age "Christ," New Age leader Barbara Marx Hubbard states:

> We *shall* all be changed.

> Those of us who are attracted to this perception of reality are like the "imaginal cells" in the body of a caterpillar when it is turning into a butterfly. As the caterpillar disintegrates, the imaginal cells hold the picture of the emerging butterfly,

and guide the formation of the new being. Similarly each of us who *knows* it is possible for the human race to evolve holds a vital facet of the picture of our metamorphosis. Like the butterfly, the emerging Whole Body of our planet is calling to us to offer our gifts freely now.[1]

In our dormant untapped creativity we shall find all the energy and knowledge required to *co-create a new world.* This is *Christ's call* to *all of us. To BE* as he is. To do as he did. This is not a dogma, it is a liberation of humanity from the *age-old trauma of separation* from God. This is the very essence of *co-creation.*[2] (emphasis added)

Advocating the occult/New Age practice of creative visualization, Hubbard's "Christ" tells everyone to *visualize* a cocoon and then to place themselves in the cocoon and his body of light:

Create the *cocoon of light.* Materialize my body of light in your mind's eye.[3] (emphasis added)

[V]isualize yourselves entering the cocoon, and placing your body in my body of light, giving it permission to become a new body like mine. It is already preprogrammed to change.[4]

In essence, the New Age "Christ" is *calling* humanity to become "a natural *Christ*"—and thus "*as he is*"—in order to *co-create* a new world of "Oneness" with him. With the light of "God" shining upon them, they will *emerge* from their *cocoons* into the "Oneness" of being self-realized gods. As seen, this false "Christ" has described this whole imaginal *co-creative* butterfly process as "*Christ's call.*" And as Tamara Hartzell has pointed out in *"Reimagining" God,* the "Jesus" of *Jesus Calling* not only speaks of *co-creating* but of this New Age concept of the "cocoon of light" as well. Sounding just like the New Age "Christ," the "Jesus" of *Jesus Calling* says:

I am all around you, like a *cocoon of Light.*[5] (emphasis added)

I, the Creator of the universe, have deigned to *co-create* with you.[6] (emphasis added)

Again, the New Age "Christ" describes what he has been doing as "Christ's call" to the world. *Christ Calling. God Calling. Jesus Calling.* All of them emphasizing in their call the importance of spiritual experience and new knowledge gained through meditation, contemplative prayer, and practicing the presence. For what purpose? To ultimately leave these caterpillar cocoon states by awakening and evolving into the "gods" that we already are and are meant to be.

Would the true Jesus Christ make the same call as the New Age "Christ" and just arbitrarily throw out parallel terms like *co-creation, quantum leap, cocoon of light,* and *divine alchemy*? No, He definitely would not.

> Woe unto them that call evil good, and good evil; that put darkness for light, and light for darkness. (Isaiah 5:20)

16

THE "GREAT WORK" OF "DIVINE ALCHEMY"

Alchemy—an ancient mystic art of the occult—is the "Great Work" of the New Age transformation, referred to as "divine alchemy." And in *Jesus Calling,* "Jesus" states:

> I can glean Joy out of sorrow, Peace out of adversity. Only a Friend who is also the King of kings could accomplish this divine alchemy.[1]

THE WORD OCCULT is defined in *Webster's New World Dictionary* as follows:

> . . . designating or of certain alleged mystic arts, such as magic, *alchemy,* astrology, etc.[2] (emphasis added)

The Oxford Classical Dictionary underscores the fact that the "art" of alchemy has serious New Age implications. The very first sentence of the definition states:

ALCHEMY in antiquity was a mixture of chemical, metallurgical, and glass technology, Greek philosophy, *mystical and syncretist religion, and astrology.*[3] (emphasis added)

Explaining the New Age/occult underpinnings of alchemy, this same *Oxford Dictionary* states:

> The art is distinguished from the pure science of chemistry by its mixture of mystical and magical elements with the technology. . . . Alchemy in late antiquity was born of the confluence of three streams: (1) *technology* . . . (2) *theory* . . . (3) *occult religion.*[4]

> The inventor was said to be Hermes [Trismegistus], and *alchemy is linked with other occult sciences* in the Hermetic literature of the first three centuries A.D., along with neo-Pythagorean, Neoplatonic, and Gnostic ideas.[5] (emphasis added)

Searching for "divine alchemy" on the Internet leads to an overwhelming number of references to the occult. In the following quote, New Age leader Marianne Williamson uses the term *divine alchemy* to refer to the very practice the "Jesus" of *Jesus Calling* is advocating:

> *Meditation* is time spent with God *in silence and quiet listening.* It is the time during which the Holy Spirit has a chance to enter into our minds and perform *His divine alchemy.*[6] (emphasis added)

In *The Revelation,* Barbara Marx Hubbard describes this alchemy as follows:

As awakening sons and daughters of God, we are *co-creators* with the energy that creates the universe. We are *new alchemists, conscious evolvers.*[7] (emphasis added)

And speaking through Hubbard, the New Age "Christ" states:

The transformation is about to begin. . . .

The *body-change*, the inner radiation which some of you now feel, is a preliminary experience to prepare you for the *alchemy* you are about to undergo.[8] (emphasis added)

The Oxford Classical Dictionary also states that ancient alchemy was often referred to as "the Work,"[9] with a capital "W." The "Jesus" of *God Calling* describes his work in several places as "My Work,"[10] also spelled with a capital "W." New Age leader Marianne Williamson has taken the term *divine alchemy* a step further when she referred to the New Age plan for the evolution of humanity as the "Great Work":

Beyond the appearances of history, there is a great and glorious unfolding plan for the destiny of nations. *According to the mystical traditions*, God carries this plan within His mind, seeking always, in every way, *channels for its furtherance.* His plan for the evolution of humanity, and the preparation of teachers to guide it, is called within the esoteric traditions *the Great Work.*[11] (emphasis added)

The two Williamson passages quoted above show how the terms *divine alchemy* and *the Great Work* are used to describe the larger New Age "plan" that is unfolding, as well as the need for "channels" to accomplish this "Great Work."

The "Lord" Maitreya—who channels through New Age leader Benjamin Creme—states that he is "the Christ" and that he is here on earth waiting for humanity to call him forth. He also uses the phrase

"Great Work" to describe his transformational divine alchemy, as he invites people to join him in this "Great Work":

> Share with Me, My friends, in a Great Work—nothing less than the transformation of this world.[12]

The "Jesus" of *God Calling* wants his listeners to "Be channels"[13] and refers to doing his "great work,"[14] and the "Jesus" of *Jesus Calling* wants his listeners to "be a channel"[15] and refers to working his "divine alchemy."[16] A "Great Work" that is carried out in the "silence" and "listening" of meditation, contemplative prayer, and practicing the presence. His work of "divine alchemy" is yet one more reason the "Jesus" of *Jesus Calling* is not to be trusted.

17

JESUS IS ABOVE ALL & "IN" ALL?

The foundational teaching of the New Age/New World Religion is that God is both *transcendent* (outside of his creation) and *immanent* (in man and all creation). Therefore, God is "in" everyone and all creation.

THE "JESUS" OF *Jesus Calling* similarly states:

I am above all, as well as *in all*.[1] (emphasis added)

But in regard to the true Jesus Christ, Scripture states:

But Jesus did not commit himself unto them, because he knew all men, And needed not that any should testify of man: for he knew what was *in* man. (John 2:24-25; emphasis added)

These two different statements must both be true *if* they are both about the true Jesus. Are we to believe the true Jesus Christ was not committed to man because He knew *He* was in man? No, as the true

Jesus Christ has made clear in Scripture, He is not "in all" as the "Jesus" claims in *Jesus Calling.*

If God is *above all* and *"in" all,* then this is *God Transcendent* and *God Immanent,* which is the foundational teaching of the New Age/New World Religion. A New World Religion that is simply waiting for the appearance of its "Christ." And this soon-to-appear Antichrist will be worshiped as the reappearance of the Christ by those whose faith is in a "God" and "Christ" that are "in" everyone. This is described in more detail in my book *False Christ Coming—Does Anybody Care?: What New Age Leaders Really Have in Store for America, the Church, and the World.*

Veteran New Age evangelist Benjamin Creme delineates the bottom-line teaching of the coming New World Religion in his book *The Reappearance of the Christ and the Masters of Wisdom.* He says:

> But eventually a new world religion will be inaugurated which will be a fusion and synthesis of the approach of the East and the approach of the West. The Christ will bring together, not simply Christianity and Buddhism, but the concept of *God transcendent*—outside of His creation— and also the concept of *God immanent* in all creation—in man and all creation.[2] (emphasis added)

Renowned theosophist and occult/New Age teacher Alice Bailey also described how this New World Religion will be founded on this same heretical teaching. She wrote:

> . . . a fresh orientation to divinity and to the acceptance of the fact of *God Transcendent* and of *God Immanent* within every form of life.
>
> These are the foundational truths upon which the world religion of the future will rest.[3] (emphasis added)

The editors of *New Age Journal* described this transcendent/immanent aspect of God and its New Age significance in their book *As Above, So Below*:

> Thousands of years ago in ancient Egypt, the great master alchemist Hermes Trismegistus, believed to be a contemporary of the Hebrew prophet Abraham, proclaimed this fundamental truth about the universe: "As above, so below; as below, so above." This maxim implies that the *transcendent* God beyond the physical universe and the *immanent* God within ourselves are one.[4] (emphasis added)

The "Jesus" of *Jesus Calling* may as well be saying, "as above, so below," when he states:

> I am above all, as well as in all.

18

Moving Toward a New Age/ New Worldview

hirley MacLaine's groundbreaking, best-selling New Age book titled *Out on a Limb* taught that we are all a part of God. Likewise, M. Scott Peck's groundbreaking, best-selling New Age book titled *The Road Less Traveled* also taught we are all a part of God.

AND THE "JESUS" of *Jesus Calling* nonchalantly told Sarah Young, and now all of her readers, to "take a road less traveled" and to "go out on a limb."

In *The Road Less Traveled*, M. Scott Peck writes:

> And again I know of no hypothesis as satisfactory as the postulation of a God who is intimately associated with us— so intimately that *He is part of us.* If you want to know the closest place to look for grace, it is within yourself. . . . To put it plainly, our unconscious is God. *God within us. We were part of God all the time.*[1] (emphasis added)

In *Out on a Limb,* Shirley MacLaine writes:

> Maybe the tragedy of the human race was that we had
> forgotten *we were each Divine.* . . . It could be that human
> beings were using their talent for complexity as an excuse to
> avoid the responsibility for being what we really understood
> we were from the beginning—basically *part of what we
> called "God.²* (emphasis added)

And in *Jesus Calling,* "Jesus" states:

> You, however, have been called to take a *"road less
> traveled."³* (emphasis added)

> Be willing to go *out on a limb* with Me. If that is where I
> am leading you, it is the safest place to be.⁴ (emphasis added)

As the church merges more and more with the spiritual language of the New Age, and also accepts New Age practices and disciplines into the church, then compromised spiritual beliefs are the result.

These two phrases "a road less traveled" and "out on a limb" can obviously be used in other contexts. However, the true Jesus Christ is quite aware of these mega best-selling New Age books. It defies reason that He would make *any* kind of positive reference—direct *or* indirect—to the titles of two of the most popular New Age books published in the last three decades. Taking "a road less traveled" with M. Scott Peck is *not* what we are called to do. Going "out on a limb" with Shirley MacLaine is *not* the safest place to be. Nor would taking "a road less traveled" and going "out on a limb" with the "Jesus" of *Jesus Calling* be a wise thing to do. There are too many occult/New Age implications.

Not that long ago, New Age terms like *ultimate reality,*[5] *universal presence,*[6] *Love-Light,*[7] *Light-bearer,*[8] *supernatural plane,*[9] *living channel,*[10] *divine alchemy,*[11] *co-create,*[12] *paradigm shift,*[13] and *true self*[14] were sure indicators of someone's New Age/metaphysical orientation.

> Not that long ago, New Age terms were sure indicators of someone's New Age/metaphysical orientation. Such terms can now be found in books like *Jesus Calling.*

All these terms can now be found in books such as *Jesus Calling* and are rapidly becoming part of the everyday language of the church. In Sarah Young's 2012 book *Jesus Today*, her "Jesus" refers to his "infinite intelligence."[15] A quick search on the Internet for the term leads to multitudinous New Age/New Thought websites. In New Age language, *infinite intelligence* refers to God "in" everyone and everything. In fact, New Age channeler Esther Hicks calls her spirit guide Abraham "Infinite Intelligence."[16]

As the church merges more and more with the spiritual language of the New Age, and also accepts New Age practices and disciplines into the church, then compromised spiritual beliefs are the result. Faith then becomes watered down, blending easily with a world where New Age beliefs are already mainstream. Ultimately, everything has to be unified for a New World Religion and a New World Order to take effect.

Webster's Dictionary defines the word *anathema* as "a solemn ecclesiastical condemnation of a teaching judged to be gravely opposed to accepted church doctrine"[17]—such as New Age teachings. But rather than declaring the teachings of the New Age "God" and "Christ" to be *anathema*, the "Jesus" of *Jesus Calling* chooses to use the word *anathema* to condemn *worrying* as "unbelief." Right before he states that "worry is a form of unbelief; it is anathema to Me," this "Jesus" begins this same paragraph with, "I am all around you, like a cocoon of Light."[18] And as we have seen, one of the teachings given by the New Age "Christ" through Barbara Marx Hubbard is "the cocoon of light."[19] Does this mean we are to believe it is anathema to "worry" about the New Age implications of the teachings of the "Jesus" of *Jesus Calling*?

In regard to worrying and having a proper worldview, this "Jesus" states:

> *The world is too much with you*, My child. Your mind leaps from problem to problem to problem, tangling your thoughts in *anxious* knots. When you think like that, you leave Me out of your *world-view* and your mind becomes darkened.[20] (emphasis added)

"The world is too much with you" is almost a direct quote from William Wordsworth's famous poem, "The World is Too Much With Us." Decrying people's worldliness, Wordsworth, a self-confessed "worshiper of Nature,"[21] spelled Nature with a capital "N" to signify God's presence "in" creation. At the end of this poem, Wordsworth rhetorically, yet forcefully, stated that he would prefer to be "[a] pagan" devoted to "a creed outworn" and behold ancient gods like Proteus or Triton than to be "out of tune" with "Nature."[22] And in his celebrated poem, "Lines Composed a Few Miles Above Tintern Abbey," Wordsworth praised the pantheistic/New Age *presence* that "rolls through all things":

> And I have felt
> *A presence* that disturbs me with the joy . . .
> A motion and a spirit, that impels
> All thinking things, all objects of all thought,
> And *rolls through all things*.[23] (emphasis added)

The question that must be asked is this: Why does the "Jesus" of *Jesus Calling* choose to quote from the equivalent of a pantheistic New Age poet to make a point about having a correct worldview?

As we have seen, this same "Jesus" who is calling those who would follow him to "take a road less traveled" and "go out on a limb" with him, also calls his followers to "seek My Presence above all else"[24] which is "My universal Presence,"[25] telling them:

> When you seek My Face, put aside thoughts of everything else. *I am above all, as well as in all.*[26] (emphasis added)

Two thousand years ago, the true Jesus Christ warned about false Christs and false teachings that would come in His name and deceive even the elect if that were possible. Two thousand years later, in *Jesus Calling*, this "Jesus" who says, "I am totally trustworthy"[27] doesn't warn about them at all. That's the *real* anathema.

19

WOULD JESUS MAGNIFY HIS PRESENCE ABOVE THE WORD OF GOD?

In *Jesus Calling*, "Jesus" promotes the experience of his presence above God's Word.

PSALM 138:2 TELLS us:

> I will worship toward thy holy temple, and praise thy name for thy lovingkindness and for thy truth: for *thou hast magnified thy word above all thy name.* (emphasis added)

Because God has magnified His Word above His name, this lets us know we will never experience *His* presence in any way that is not totally consistent with the truth of His Word. Thus, we can know that *any* presence that comes calling and claims the name of "Jesus" as its own but does not line up *in every way* with God's *Word* is not the presence of *God*. God will never put His name or experiencing His presence above His Word.

The true Jesus Christ tells us:

Heaven and earth shall pass away, but my words shall not pass away. (Matthew 24:35)

God is always present with us—a presence that will never be magnified above His Word. If we choose to put experiencing God's presence above His Word, we are leaving ourselves open and vulnerable to the visits of a counterfeit presence.

For the "Jesus" of *Jesus Calling*, experiencing His presence is everything. This is his invitation:

> Open yourself to My loving Presence, so that I may fill you with My fullness. I want you to experience *how wide and long and high and deep is My Love for you, so that you can know My Love that surpasses knowledge.* This vast ocean of Love cannot be measured or explained, but it can be experienced.[1]

> *Taste and see that I am good.* This command contains an invitation to experience My living Presence. It also contains a promise. The more you experience Me, the more convinced you become of My goodness.[2]

It is not surprising that a counterfeit presence will emphasize its own presence *above* the Word of God because the Word of God is where we find the truth of God. And this false Christ uses Psalm 34:8 which says, "O taste and see that the LORD is good," to make the case for "tasting" his *presence*. But as we see in Psalm 119:103-104, we are to "taste" the *Word of God*:

> How sweet are *thy words* unto my *taste*! yea, sweeter than honey to my mouth! Through thy precepts I get understanding: therefore I hate every false way. (emphasis added)

Also, we are told in the next verse of this Psalm:

Thy word is a lamp unto my feet, and a light unto my path. (Psalm 119:105)

It is *God's Word* that is the light of our path—a light in which we can clearly see that a presence is counterfeit. It is for good reason that God will never put His name or experiencing His presence above the light of His Word. But in *Jesus Calling*, "Jesus" goes out of his way to promote the experience of his presence—an experience that lets the "Light" of his presence "soak into you" as a substitute for the revealing light of God's Word:

My Word is a lamp to your feet; *My Presence* is a Light for your path.[3] (emphasis added)

Let *the Light of My Presence* soak into you, as you focus your thoughts on Me. Thus I equip you to face whatever the day brings.[4] (emphasis added)

It is in the revealing light of God's Word that the true Jesus Christ warns:

Take heed therefore that the light which is in thee be not darkness. (Luke 11:35)

However, the "Jesus" that comes calling as an "abiding Presence" wants to "soak" you with the light that is dark. And he says:

My abiding Presence is the best road map available.[5] (emphasis added)

Begin each day anticipating problems, asking Me to equip you for whatever difficulties you will encounter. *The best equipping is My living Presence.*[6] (emphasis added)

You need the certainty of My loving Presence in order to weather the storms of life. During times of severe testing, *even the best theology can fail you* if it isn't accompanied by *experiential knowledge of Me.*[7] (emphasis added)

But Scripture tells us:

All scripture is given by inspiration of God, and is profitable for doctrine, for reproof, for correction, for instruction in righteousness: That the man of God may be perfect, thoroughly furnished unto all good works. (2 Timothy 3:16-17)

As mentioned, the word "Presence" is found more than 365 times in *Jesus Calling*. And in both *God Calling* and *Jesus Calling*, "Jesus" states that experiencing his presence will unlock secret teachings, new revelations, and future things to come. The "Jesus" of *God Calling* states:

For you, My children, I will unlock the *secret* treasures hidden from so many.[8] (emphasis added)

You must ponder on these truths I give you. They are not surface facts, but the *secrets* of My Kingdom, the hidden pearls of rare price.[9] (emphasis added)

And the "Jesus" of *Jesus Calling* states:

Instead, I will lead you along fresh trails of adventure, *revealing to you things you did not know.* Stay in communication with Me. Follow My guiding Presence.[10] (emphasis added)

As you follow Me, I lead you along paths of *newness:* ways you have never imagined.[11] (emphasis added)

Sarah Young wanted "more" than what was communicated in God's Word—and "more" is exactly what she got. It would seem that "a word from God" became more important than the Word of God. This yearning for "more" is what helped open her up to experiencing a presence that is only too glad to give her its *new* revelations and *new* truths. She writes in *Jesus Calling*:

> The following year, I began to wonder if I, too, could receive messages during my times of communing with God. I had been writing in prayer journals for years, but that was one-way communication: I did all the talking. *I knew that God communicated with me through the Bible, but I yearned for more.* Increasingly, I wanted to hear what God had to say to me personally on a given day. I decided to listen to God with pen in hand, writing down whatever I believed He was saying.[12] (emphasis added)

The presence that came calling on Sarah Young is extending an invitation to the readers of *Jesus Calling* to experience his presence as well—an invitation that is depicted in the book cover's *inviting hand*. Keep in mind that another invitation is also taking place. If we choose to sit "with pen in hand" waiting to hear "more" than God's inspired Holy Word, we, too, have an *inviting hand*. But what presence are we actually inviting into our lives?

If one becomes dependent on a subjective presence rather than the objective Holy Bible, deception is inevitable. That is why it is crucial to compare what is taught by anyone or anything to the revealing light of God's Word. *Test the spirits* of any presence that may appear in your devotions and quiet times.

> Study to shew thyself approved unto God, a workman that needeth not to be ashamed, rightly dividing the word of truth. (2 Timothy 2:15)

20

"ANOTHER JESUS" CALLING

T he presence of the "Jesus" of *Jesus Calling* has captivated millions of readers, mixing truth and error.

IN DR. HARRY IRONSIDE'S article titled "Exposing Error: Is it Worthwhile?," he writes:

> Error is like leaven, of which we read, "A little leaven leaveneth the whole lump." Truth mixed with error is equivalent to all error, except that it is more innocent looking and, therefore, more dangerous. God hates such a mixture! Any error, or any truth-and-error mixture, calls for definite exposure and repudiation. To condone such is to be unfaithful to God and His Word and treacherous to imperiled souls for whom Christ died."[1]

When I expressed my concerns about *Jesus Calling* to a church group in Calgary, Alberta, a distraught woman approached me afterwards. She just couldn't believe there might be something wrong with the book. She said she loved *Jesus Calling* and was reading it daily. A man in Appleton, Wisconsin, shared with me that he and a number of people in his church had been fooled because they assumed that *Jesus Calling* had to be biblical because there were Scripture references at the bottom of each page. When I gave a talk in New Orleans, Louisiana, at a home Bible study group, one of the attendees told me that four different people had given her a copy of *Jesus Calling*. She said she stopped reading the book after just a few pages because she knew something wasn't right. A woman I know in Southern California told a friend that *Jesus Calling* had some serious problems, but before she could say anything further, her friend told her that she didn't want to hear it. The friend was very clear—"Don't even go there!" A young woman in Northern California who initially loved *Jesus Calling* ultimately abandoned the book. The following is her written account of the experience:

> I was given *Jesus Calling* as a gift from a friend who had previously shared what I was suffering: postpartum depression. She claimed this book would help me and bring me peace.
>
> I found peace in Sarah Young's book. Every day's devotion was a new light for me that invited a new presence in my home; Jesus' presence. This new (Jesus) presence that I was reading about [seemed] more powerful than the God of the Bible. I remember thinking "this is not the Jesus I know." I was so enamored and fixed on this peace, and his presence, and the picture of his hand on the cover of the book that I started imagining God (literally) walking by my side everywhere I went. I started putting the devotions above God's Word and would justify to myself that each devotion was more powerful than reading God's Word. This peace I thought I had was so convincing and real that I thought I had found a better way to read God's Word. I remember God's Holy Spirit speaking to me during

these months of False peace by putting this question in my mind—"Is this book above the Bible?" or "Is this book more important than my Word?"

Once I realized that I had defiled God's presence with a false book, I understood that the Jesus in *Jesus Calling* was not the Jesus of Christianity or my fearful God that the Bible talks about, but a God whom I imagined to be my equal.[2]

At the top of her written account, she cited the following two verses:

I am sought of them that asked not for me; I am found of them that sought me not: I said, Behold me, behold me, unto a nation that was not called by my name. (Isaiah 65:1)

For false Christs and false prophets shall rise, and shall shew signs and wonders, to seduce, if it were possible, even the elect. (Mark 13:22)

When also summarizing her experience with our mutual friend, Tamara Hartzell, this same young woman spoke the following thoughts:

I had kept on trying to search for what Jesus looks like and who God is. And it was like *Jesus Calling* took the Jesus of the Bible and made Him look like nothing compared to the Jesus of *Jesus Calling*. It was like the book made Him more powerful and amplified His power tenfold. It was just an overwhelming powerful feeling. And it was all in the way the devotional was worded. It was the Jesus I was looking for, that I wanted, that could make everything perfect.

There were certain passages in the book that made me question who God was—it was a different God than the God of

> "The book made me think I was special, that God would want me in His presence. It made me feel supernatural, like I could do anything because God was standing right next to me. It was the most peaceful feeling."

the Bible. This God of *Jesus Calling* is more powerful in giving you what you want and in easing my burdens.

This make-believe God was who I wanted God to be. The book set you up to believe in a God that is bigger than the God of the Bible. That you can then imagine Him to look like whatever you wanted Him to look like.

The book made me think I was special, that God would want me in His presence. It made me feel supernatural, like I could do anything because God was standing right next to me. It was the most peaceful feeling.

It was a very strong peace like ecstasy that wouldn't last.

It drew me in more to wanting God's presence. I didn't want God's presence to leave. It was a very powerful, spiritual presence. I would go back and re-read January and February and March just so I could feel God's presence.

It was like taking God down from heaven and putting Him in the room with me. That's how I felt.

I felt like God was standing right next to me and in the room with me. I felt like I was equal with God and some spiritual person.

It separated me from everyone else. The book makes you feel like you're this chosen one, and super special.

I kept envisioning God right next to me and walking with me in my home. I had no fear of Him and felt like He was my equal—because He could walk with me in my home. It was great. He would go with me to church and I felt like He was sitting next to me and not anyone else. Then I started thinking about it, and said wait a second, this isn't right.

The book has power over you, definitely. When you open the book there is overwhelming power. I can't believe I thought it had more power than the Bible. And I wouldn't read my Bible for a long time.

I just knew that the Spirit that was ministering to me out of the book was not the same Spirit that was ministering to [convicting] my heart. I got more peace out of reading that book than I got out of reading the Bible and that really scared me.[3]

And as the young woman stated in her written account, she eventually "understood that the Jesus in *Jesus Calling* was not the Jesus of Christianity." Thus, she stopped reading *Jesus Calling* after she realized she was being deceived by both the book and the spiritual experiences that came with it. But this young woman's response is *not* typical of those reading *Jesus Calling*.

The presence of this "Jesus" has captivated millions of readers as he seems to meet people right where they are at. Blending his words with those of Scripture, he exhorts *Jesus Calling* readers to let *his* presence be your "guide,"[4] let *his* presence "control your mind"[5] and "reprogram your thinking,"[6] let *his* presence "invade" your life[7] and be your "all"[8] as he tells you to "[l]augh at the future"[9] and assures you that "all is well."[10] But all is *not* well if this presence is not the true Jesus Christ.

In today's world, there are many false "Christs" seeking our devotion. But there will come that moment when the *true* Christ will appear, and those who are following a false "Christ" will find out they have been deceived. Yet perhaps the most amazing thing about all this is that we have the opportunity *right now*—while there is still time—to pray and ask God to correct us if we are *in any way* being deceived. And we need to test the spirits just as the Bible instructs us to do.

It is a very humbling experience to realize that you have been deceived. However, with that realization comes a deep appreciation for the literal Word of God—how in addition to God's love and mercy, it warns about the reality of spiritual deception, seducing spirits, false prophets, false teachers, false Christs, persecution, contending for the faith, fighting the good fight, and enduring to the end. The Bible doesn't flatter the reader or water down the truth—it tells it like it is and lays it right on the line.

What it all comes down to is this: Do we have a love of the truth or do we just experience what we want to experience and hear what we want to hear? Ultimate truth is not found in channeled messages, "new" revelations, or "new" truth. Ultimate truth—God's truth and nothing but God's truth—is explicitly, authoritatively, genuinely, and most amazingly found in the pages of God's inspired Holy Word. And it is in those pages that we find our wonderful Lord and Savior Jesus Christ.

A tremendous spiritual deception is going on in the world and in the church. You don't want to be part of it. If you are willing, humble yourself before your Maker and pray to the true God in the name of the true Savior Jesus Christ, and ask Him to let you know if you are being deceived by "another Jesus," "another spirit," or "another gospel."

EPILOGUE

NOT LONG AFTER our conversion, my wife and I sat down one day and talked about the ultimate spiritual deception described in the Bible—the great "falling away" of the church and the coming of Antichrist. We agreed that for someone like Antichrist to be credible in the world, he would need a majority of the people who call themselves Christians to believe that he was Christ. If he could get enough Christians—especially Christian leaders—to follow him, he could then discredit and marginalize those who opposed him. But to get people who call themselves Christians to believe that he was Christ, he would first have to successfully redefine Christianity. To do that he would have to introduce non-Christian teachings and practices into the church, while at the same time make them *seem* Christian. His obvious goal would be to convert undiscerning and unsuspecting believers into a more eastern/mystical New Age "Christianity." While invoking the name of "God" and "Christ" he would actually turn the Bible upside down—just as we had seen in *A Course in Miracles* and in our other New Age teachings. Christianity would become a more "positive" New Age Christianity. This *emerging* New Age Christianity would have "a form of godliness" but it would actually deny the true faith (2 Timothy 3:5). This New Age Christianity/New Spirituality would use Christian terminology but it would be under the spell of "another Jesus," "another spirit," and "another gospel" (2 Corinthians 11:4). This New Age/New Gospel/New Spirituality would be the ultimate counterfeit and the ultimate deception. It would be what the true Jesus warned his followers to watch out for.

MEDITATION AND CONTEMPLATION

THE New Age/New Spirituality has made great inroads into the church—particularly in the area of meditation and contemplative prayer. Despite grave warnings from many of us who came out of the New Age movement, the church remains extremely vulnerable to deceptive supernatural experiences that *appear* to come from God.

We knew from our own New Age involvement that powerful, seemingly "meant to be" spiritual experiences had often been used to draw us into the New Age and its various spiritual practices, which included meditation and contemplation. And we knew that the same seductive experiences, which had led us into the New Age, continued *within* our meditations and contemplations. Because our spiritual experiences felt so good, we just assumed that what we were experiencing was coming from God. Our spiritual practices soon became the primary connecting force that gave us "the feeling" we were on the right track. These daily meditations and contemplations served to reinforce our emerging New Age beliefs, and had the effect of leading us deeper and deeper into the teachings of the New Age/New Spirituality.

For most of us in the New Age, meditation was an integral part of daily life. Because it was so relaxing and felt so good, we, like Sarah Young and her readers, had no idea that our meditations and contemplations were opening us up to great deception. Looking back on it now, meditation was the major pipeline through which deceptive spirits impressed upon us their New Age thoughts and teachings. The spiritual "high" that often accompanied our meditations and contemplations even seemed to corroborate the teaching of the New Age that we were all "one" because God was "in" everyone and everything. In fact, in my very first meditation, I experienced a "mysterious sense of oneness" that I perceived to be my "divine connection" to that oneness. One of the daily lessons I contemplated from *A Course in Miracles* was: "Let me remember I am one with God."[1]

Ironically, even biblical meditation can be manipulated into a form of New Age contemplative prayer. One of the clever ploys of our spiritual Adversary has been to repackage eastern/mystical New

Age meditation as "Christian" meditation and contemplation. In his powerful book *Death of a Guru: A Hindu Comes to Christ*, former Hindu Rabrindranath R. Maharaj describes how even seemingly benign and relaxing forms of meditation and contemplation can be used by the spirit world to provide an experience of cosmic oneness:

> Though popularized in the West under many names, the aim of all Eastern meditation is to "realize" one's essential union with the Universe. It is the doorway to the "nothingness" called nirvana. Generally sold as a "relaxation" technique, meditation really aims at and ultimately leads to the surrender of oneself to mystical cosmic forces.[2]

BARBARA MARX HUBBARD'S CONTEMPLATIVE PRAYER

BIBLICAL meditation is generally understood to be when one prayerfully and thoughtfully considers a passage of Scripture. Unfortunately, many who think they are practicing biblical meditation confusedly cross over into unbiblical, eastern/mystical New Age meditation. This is often described as contemplative prayer and may even begin with contemplating Scripture. But contemplating or meditating on Scripture does not guarantee that what follows is necessarily from God. Scripture in and of itself doesn't offer protection—especially if you enter into "the silence" and just assume that what you are experiencing or hearing is definitely from God.

A perfect example is what happened to former seeker, but now New Age leader, Barbara Marx Hubbard. After she "contemplated" a passage from Scripture, she received a powerful vision that propelled her into the New Age/New Spirituality belief system and eventually into New Age leadership. In her book *The Revelation*, she describes what took place after "contemplating" 1 Corinthians 12:12. Because of the magnitude of the spiritual deception, I have quoted from her at length:

On a fateful afternoon in February 1966, I was taking my usual daily walk. . . .

I had been reading Reinhold Neibuhr on the subject of community. He had quoted St. Paul's famous statement: "For as the body is one, and hath many members, and all the members of that one body, being many, are one body, so also is Christ." As I contemplated that idea, I felt a deep frustration. . . .

Unexpectedly a new question burst forth in my mind. I spoke it out loud. Lifting my voice to the ice-white sky, I demanded to know:

"What is our story? What in our age is comparable to the birth of Christ?" . . .

I lapsed into a daydreamlike state . . . I was poised from within, to catch the slightest hint of revelation.

Suddenly my mind's eye penetrated beyond the blue cocoon of Earth, lifting me up into the utter blackness of outer space. From there I witnessed the entire sweep of Earth's history, as though I were viewing a technicolor movie.

I witnessed the Earth as a living body . . . I felt myself to be a cell in that body. . . .

Then the movie sped up. I saw something new. A flash of extraordinary light more radiant than the sun surrounded the planet. Instantly, all of us were attracted to the light. We forgot our pain, and at that moment of shared attention, empathy began to course through our planetary body. Wave upon wave of love flowed through all people. A magnetic field of love aligned us. We were caressed, uplifted in this field of light. We felt our inner light rising. Mass healings occurred. People flooded out of their houses, offices, and buildings, meeting each other in ever-growing gatherings, embracing, loving one another. . . .

Then I heard the inner words clearly:

Our story is a birth. It is the birth of humankind as one body. . . .

In response to those words, which had seemed to come from deep within the universe, billions of us opened our collective eyes and smiled. It was a Planetary Smile. . . . Ecstatic joy rippled through the planetary body . . . and through me as one of its billions of members.[3]

All of this "new revelation"—the very foundation of Hubbard's New Age ministry today—came after Hubbard "contemplated" a single verse from the Bible: 1 Corinthians 12:12. But supernatural experiences are obviously not from God if they contradict His written Word. Not being a Christian and not knowing how to test the spirits, she opened herself up to spiritual deception.

While most of us in the New Age didn't have Hubbard's extreme spiritual experience, we had our own versions. And what we were being taught through our spiritual experiences was that our experience should take precedence over any written word or any prior beliefs. In fact, we were told that our spiritual experiences should provide the foundation for new beliefs. And most often these experiences would come during periods of meditation and contemplation.

HUBBARD'S BIBLICAL MEDITATION

IT should be carefully noted that as a spiritual seeker, Hubbard had been greatly deceived after uttering a contemplative prayer that had focused on Scripture. She would also later describe how she started to "regularly" hear an "inner voice" after learning to say the Lord's Prayer in deep concentration during meditation:

> In 1977 I began to meditate, going to the hill behind my home in Washington D.C. each morning. I learned to say the Lord's Prayer in deep concentration. I started to hear regularly an inner voice.[4]

This "inner voice" was to become Hubbard's "Christ voice."[5] She explained how her "inner voice" transformed itself into the "Christ voice" during a silent retreat at the Mount Calvary Episcopal Monastery in Santa Barbara, California, in 1980. The monastery had described the weekend as a "non directed weekend of silence open to everyone, to renew inner peace and meet the Lord in the monastic round of Offices, Eucharist, quiet and nonverbal fellowship."[6] Hubbard told how she encountered the "Christ voice" as she sat in silence beneath a wooden cross at the monastery:

> Early in the morning, as I was sitting beneath a little wooden cross upon the top of the hill, overlooking the world below, the inner voice guided me as I wrote in my journal.[7]

> Then the "voice," which until now had seemed to be my own higher self, became elevated and was transformed into an even higher voice, the Christ voice. I felt an electrifying presence of light, a field that lifted me up.[8]

It was at this Episcopal monastery that Hubbard, under the direction of her "Christ," rewrote parts of the New Testament and began to describe a New Age "Christianity" that mandated a belief in the "Christ within," as well as a "selection process" to select out those who refused to believe in their own divinity.[9]

For those who believe that solitude, silence, contemplative prayer, or even "Christian" meditation are the sole province of God, Barbara

Marx Hubbard remains a good example of why they had better think again. Hubbard's serious contemplation of 1 Corinthians 12:12 and the Lord's Prayer did not prevent her from being spiritually deceived. What happened to Hubbard, and what happened to so many of us in the New Age—and even to Johanna Michaelsen and Sarah Young—can happen to *anyone* who chooses to believe personal spiritual experience over God's written Word. It can happen to *anyone* who does not test the spirits of what they are experiencing (Hebrews 4:12; 1 John 4:1-3).

> Be sober, be vigilant; because your adversary the devil, as a roaring lion, walketh about, seeking whom he may devour. (1 Peter 5:8)

CHANGING JESUS CALLING: DAMAGE CONTROL FOR A FALSE CHRIST

PUBLISHER PROBLEMS

WHAT IF YOU are a major publisher like Thomas Nelson and you suddenly discover that your mega best-selling book *Jesus Calling* was inspired by a channeled New Age book? And what if you find out that some of the "messages" your author "received" from her "Jesus" weren't really from Jesus because they contradict what the real Jesus Christ says in the Bible? And what if your best-selling author has introduced a host of other problems in her book that your usually sharp editors had somehow overlooked? What do you do given these issues are already in the pages of ten million previously published books? If you want to be fair to your readers, you deal honestly with these problems as they are brought to your attention. However, if you are more interested in protecting your product rather than in protecting the truth, you do everything in your power to make these problems disappear. One thing is for sure. Sarah Young and Thomas Nelson have made some of their problems suddenly disappear in recent editions of *Jesus Calling—*

most especially in a special 10th anniversary edition of *Jesus Calling* released on September 30, 2014.

LIKE THE WATERGATE TAPES

PERHAPS taking their cue from the missing eighteen-and-a-half minutes from Richard Nixon's Watergate tapes, Sarah Young and Thomas Nelson have been systematically deleting controversial material from *Jesus Calling*. Adding, subtracting, cutting, pasting, and completely eliminating problematic words, sentences, and even whole paragraphs, Young and her editors do not hesitate to put words in the mouth of their "Jesus," even as they take others away. But like the Watergate tapes, the missing evidence and their in-your-face tactics are doing more to expose their problems than cover them up.

"ANOTHER JESUS" CALLING

IN the fall of 2013, my book *"Another Jesus" Calling* was published by Lighthouse Trails Publishing. I was not the first person to express concern about *Jesus Calling*, but not much had been written up to that point. As our concerns were publicized, Sarah Young and Thomas Nelson obviously became aware of our objections. Without a word of explanation to anyone, significant alterations have been made to recent editions of *Jesus Calling*. With "now you see it, now you don't" editing, some of their major problems suddenly disappeared from the pages of *Jesus Calling*. To illustrate the lengths to which Sarah Young and Thomas Nelson have gone to protect their book and their multi-million dollar *Jesus Calling* industry, I will provide five specific examples—and there are many others—to demonstrate how readers of *Jesus Calling* are being managed and manipulated. Make no mistake about it—damage control is in full swing at Thomas Nelson, and it is especially evident in their special 10th anniversary edition of Sarah Young's book.

FIVE PROBLEMS

1) *JESUS CALLING* WAS INSPIRED BY A CHANNELED NEW AGE BOOK

Jesus Calling was inspired by the book *God Calling.*[1] In an interview with the Christian Broadcasting Network, author Sarah Young said that her journey with *Jesus Calling* began with the book *God Calling.* She stated:

> My journey began with a devotional book (*God Calling*) written in the 1930s by two women who practiced waiting in God's Presence, writing the messages they received as they "listened." About a year after I started reading this book, I began to wonder if I too could receive messages during my times of communing with God. . . . So I decided to "listen" to God with pen in hand, writing down whatever I sensed He was saying.[2] (parenthesis in original)

But Sarah Young and her editors somehow missed the fact that *God Calling* is a channeled New Age book. *God Calling* is a collection of channeled messages presented in the form of a daily devotional. The messages were channeled through two English women in the 1930s and could easily have been titled *Jesus Calling* because it was reputedly dictated by "The Living Christ Himself."[3]

The Encyclopedia of New Age Beliefs, published by Harvest House Christian publishers, specifically describes *God Calling* as a channeled New Age book. In their lengthy chapter on channeling and spiritual dictation, authors/apologists John Weldon and John Ankerberg explain that channeling is a form of New Age "mediumship" and according to the Bible it "is a practice forbidden (Deuteronomy 18:9-12)."[4] Under the subheading titled "Impersonations of Christianity," the authors describe *God Calling* as a New Age book "replete with denials of biblical teaching"[5] as it "subtly encourages psychic development and spiritistic inspiration under the guise of Christ's personal guidance . . . and often misinterprets Scripture."[6] Yet Sarah Young wrote that it was *God Calling* that inspired her to receive her own messages from "Jesus." In her original introduction to *Jesus Calling*, Young praised *God Calling* as "a treasure to me":

> During that same year **I began reading *God Calling*,** a devotional book written by two anonymous "listeners." These women practiced waiting quietly in God's Presence, pencils and paper in hand, recording the messages they received from Him. The messages are written in first person, with "I" designating God. While I was living in Japan, someone had mailed this book to me from the U.S. I had not read it at that time, but I had held onto the book through two international moves. Six or seven years later, **this little paperback became a treasure to me**. It dove-tailed remarkably well with my longing to live in Jesus' Presence.[7] (bold added)

THE DAMAGE CONTROL

In recent editions of *Jesus Calling*—including the 10th anniversary edition—the preceding paragraph regarding *God Calling* has been removed from the author's longstanding introduction. No explanation. No apology. Nothing. Suddenly and completely gone is any mention of *God Calling*—how it had inspired her to receive her own "messages" from "Jesus" and how it was a "treasure" to her. Her previous praise of *God Calling* had become problematic as it had drawn obvious New Age comparisons to her own book. It had also become apparent that her original endorsement of *God Calling* was helping to popularize this New Age book among believers!

While Christian leaders have been strangely silent about *Jesus Calling*, it was the secular media that took Sarah Young and Thomas

Nelson to task for changing and deleting problematic material in their best-selling book. Ruth Graham, writing in *The Daily Beast*, a popular online American news reporting and opinion website formerly associated with *Newsweek* magazine, wrote an article questioning the changes being made to Sarah Young's original introduction. Graham wrote:

> The latest edition of *Jesus Calling* includes some important changes. The paragraph about *God Calling* has been deleted, and references to received "messages" have been changed to the less mystically inflected "writings and devotions." In a passage in which Young recounts her early attempts to write down what God told her, the new version characterizes this as "focusing on Jesus and His Word, while asking Him to guide my thoughts." Thomas Nelson refers to the book as "Sarah's prayer journal," emphasizing that Young is not claiming to speak for Jesus. A skeptical reader, comparing the two introductions, would see an effort by a publisher to bring an increasingly controversial but lucrative best-seller into line with mainstream evangelical orthodoxy.[8]

In that same article, Ruth Graham also questioned the explanations offered by Thomas Nelson publicist Katie Powell:

> In an email responding to my questions, the book's publicist at Thomas Nelson, Katie Powell, wrote that the reference to *God Calling* was never meant as more than "a nod," and it was deleted because it had "created some confusion." "The book's theology has always been sound," she wrote. "The changes were made to make the introduction easier to understand, especially since *Jesus Calling* is now being read by such a wide variety of people." Thomas Nelson did not call attention to the changes, Powell wrote, because the introduction's

"content did not change" between editions. But it's hard to square that with the similarities between Young's book and *God Calling*—right down to the title.[9]

Graham's skepticism is right on target. And contrary to the statement by the Thomas Nelson publicist, the content of the introduction *has* changed in recent editions. The unexplained changes have caused many former supporters of *Jesus Calling* to stop using the devotional. Christian online newspaper *WorldNetDaily* (*WND*) picked up on the controversy and published two articles,"Top Christian Bestseller Accused of Heresy"[10] and "Is Hit Book '*Jesus Calling*' Pushing New Age?"[11] *Charisma* magazine followed up with a similar article that noted the growing controversy. It was titled "Critics Accuse '*Jesus Calling*' of Mixing Truth With New Age Error."[12]

Note: For Sarah Young to not have initially recognized *God Calling* as a New Age book should raise some serious red flags. For her to praise *God Calling* as "a treasure to me" should raise those red flags even further. But for Sarah Young and her publisher to remove all references to *God Calling* without any explanation or apology to her millions of readers is perhaps the reddest flag of all. It is the height of spiritual irresponsibility for Sarah Young to pretend it is no big deal after her original endorsement of *God Calling* re-ignited the sales of this blatant New Age book, especially when *God Calling*—thanks to her—now sits alongside *Jesus Calling* in thousands of bookstores across the country—including countless Christian bookstores.

2) SARAH YOUNG ORIGINALLY WROTE THAT SHE "RECEIVED MESSAGES" FROM "JESUS" HIMSELF

Because of Sarah Young's stated affection for the channeled "messages" in *God Calling,* the "messages" she was receiving from "Jesus" were immediately suspect.

THE DAMAGE CONTROL

In recent editions of *Jesus Calling*, all ten references to the words "message" and "messages" have been deleted from her otherwise longstanding introduction. What were originally described as "messages" she "received" from "Jesus" are now being described as "writings" and "devotions" that she "gleaned" in her "quiet moments."

- **Sentences in Her Original Introduction**
  This practice of listening to God has increased my intimacy with Him more than any other spiritual discipline, **so I want to share some of the messages I have received.** In many parts of the world, Christians seem to be searching for a deeper experience of Jesus' Presence and Peace. **The messages that follow** address that felt need.[13] (bold added)

- **Replacement Sentences in Recent Editions**
  This practice of being still in God's Presence has increased my intimacy with Him more than any other spiritual discipline, **so I want to share some of the writings I have gleaned from these quiet moments.** In many parts of the world, Christians seem to be searching for a deeper experience of Jesus' Presence and Peace. **The devotions that follow** address that felt need.[14] (bold added)

In the example immediately below, observe how "messages" again become "devotions" in the replacement sentence now found in recent editions. Also note how the phrase "with your Bible open" has been added to the original wording to make things appear more biblical.

- **Sentence in Her Original Introduction**
  These messages are meant to be read slowly, preferably in a quiet place.[15] (bold added)

• **Replacement Sentence in Recent Editions**
The devotions in this book are meant to be read slowly, preferably in a quiet place—with your Bible open.[16] (bold added)

Note: In the not yet damage-controlled original introduction to *Jesus Calling: 365 Devotions for Kids*, Sarah Young makes it abundantly clear that what she calls "devotions" are in fact "messages" she has "received" from her "Jesus." She writes:

> Since then, I have practiced listening a lot. Usually I write His messages in a notebook, but sometimes I just spend time with Him for a while—and write nothing. The devotions in this book **are some of the messages** I have received.[17] (bold added)

Note: Changing the "messages" she "received" to the "writings" and "devotions" she "gleaned" in her "quiet moments" attempts to counter any suggestion that Sarah Young might be getting deceived by a seducing spirit that is presenting itself as the real Jesus (1 Timothy 4:1, Matthew 24:4-5).

3) SARAH YOUNG'S "JESUS" CONTRADICTS THE BIBLE'S TRUE JESUS CHRIST

In two separate messages, Sarah Young was told by her "Jesus" that the last words he spoke after his resurrection and before ascending into heaven were "I am with you always." But this statement made by the true Jesus Christ on the Mount of Galilee were not His last words before ascending into heaven. His last words were spoken from the Mount of Olives as recorded in Acts 1:7-9, 12. The two "messages" Sarah Young received from *her* "Jesus" contradict the words of the true Jesus Christ in the Holy Bible. What her "Jesus" said was totally unbiblical.

THE DAMAGE CONTROL

Since this unbiblical contradiction was brought to light in my book *"Another Jesus" Calling*, Sarah Young and Thomas Nelson have eliminated this obvious contradiction in their 10th anniversary edition. In other words, they had their "Jesus" correct himself. Compare the original January 28th and October 15th statements that have been in *Jesus Calling* for the last ten years, with the replacement statements now inserted in the new 10th anniversary edition.

- **January 28th Original Statement**
I AM WITH YOU ALWAYS. **These were the last words** I spoke **before ascending into heaven**. I continue to proclaim this promise to all who will listen.[18] (bold added)

- **January 28th Replacement Statement**
I AM WITH YOU ALWAYS. I spoke these words to My disciples **after My resurrection.** I continue to proclaim this promise to all who will listen.[19] (bold added)

- **October 15th Original Statement**
TRY TO STAY CONSCIOUS OF ME as you go step by step through this day. My Presence with you is both a promise and a protection. **My final statement just before I went to heaven** was: Surely I am with you always. That promise was for all of My followers, without exception.[20] (bold added)

- **October 15th Replacement Statement**
TRY TO STAY CONSCIOUS OF ME as you go step by step through this day. My Presence with you is both a promise and a protection. **After My resurrection,** I assured My followers: Surely I am with you always. That promise was for all of My followers, without exception.[21] (bold added)

Note: One of the 250 "messages" Sarah Young included in her yet-to-be-corrected *Jesus Calling Devotional Bible* (*NKJV*) is the original October 15ᵗʰ "message" from *Jesus Calling*—"My final statement just before I went to heaven was: Surely I am with you always." Given that this statement is clearly unbiblical, Young's justification for her messages to be included "alongside the biblical text" falls a little flat. She writes:

> Since my writings are rooted in the infallible, unchanging Word of God, having them appear alongside the biblical text would seem to be a natural place for them.[22]

JESUS CORRECTS HIMSELF?

SARAH Young might argue that because Jesus never contradicts Himself, she must have heard it wrong. But if that were the case, she had to hear it wrong on two separate occasions because the unbiblical statement is in two different messages. With this in mind, an important question must be asked. Who was Sarah Young listening to when she "received" these two "messages?" Obviously the real Jesus does not contradict Himself—much less correct Himself in regards to His own words and actions.

And for those who might argue that there is no longer a problem because this contradiction and other problematic areas have been corrected, several more questions must be asked. What about the ten million readers who have trusted these unbiblical messages over the last ten years? Do you just pretend it never happened? Aren't they owed some kind of explanation as to how Sarah Young's "Jesus" could make mistakes of this magnitude. But perhaps most importantly, how can an author and publisher—or anyone for that matter—believe they have the right to put words in and out of the mouth of Jesus Christ like He is some kind of literary device—and most especially when it is for the purpose of damage control?

Regardless of whether Sarah Young has been listening to a deceptive spirit (1 Timothy 4:1) or to her own confused thoughts (1 Corinthians 14:33)—or a combination of both—she is deceived and is, in turn, deceiving others (2 Timothy 3:13) whether she realizes it or not. Believers must search the Scriptures to see if the things they are being told are really true (Acts 17:11), and they must test the voices they are listening to "because many false prophets are gone out into the world" (1 John 4:1).

4) SARAH YOUNG'S "JESUS" STATED THAT ABRAHAM WAS GUILTY OF "IDOLATRY" AND "SON-WORSHIP"

Sarah Young's "Jesus" said that Abraham was a man of "undisciplined emotions" and was guilty of "son-worship" and "idolatry." Many believers have recoiled at these strange, extra-biblical remarks.

THE DAMAGE CONTROL

Sarah Young and Thomas Nelson have attempted to make this particular problem disappear by deleting all references to Abraham and Isaac in the August 23rd message in recent editions of *Jesus Calling*. As they eliminate Abraham and Isaac, they are simultaneously cutting, pasting, and inserting Jacob and Joseph in their place. Compare the original August 23rd entry with the one that has replaced it in recent editions.

> • **August 23rd "Message" in the Original Edition**
> ENTRUST YOUR LOVED ONES TO ME; release them into My protective care. They are much safer with Me than in your clinging hands. If you let a loved one become an idol in your heart, you endanger that one—as well as yourself. **Remember the extreme measures I used with Abraham and Isaac. I took Isaac to the very point of death to free Abraham from son-worship. Both Abraham and Isaac suffered terribly because of the father's undisciplined emotions.** I detest idolatry, even in the form of parental love.[23] (bold added and signifies material that was deleted)

- **August 23rd Replacement Message**

ENTRUST YOUR LOVED ONES TO ME; release them into My protective care. They are much safer with Me than in your clinging hands. If you let a loved one become an idol in your heart, you endanger that one—as well as yourself. **Joseph and his father, Jacob, suffered terribly because Jacob loved Joseph more than any of his other sons and treated him with special favor. So Joseph's brothers hated him and plotted against him. Ultimately, I used that situation for good, but both father and son had to endure years of suffering and separation from one another.**

I detest idolatry, even in the form of parental love, so beware of making a beloved child your idol.[24] (bold added and signifies material that was added)

Note: Sarah Young and her editors obviously made a determination that substituting a toned down Jacob and Joseph entry would be more plausible than the original Abraham and Isaac message. However, the obvious cut-and-paste damage control has resulted in bringing more attention rather than less to their extra-biblical problem.

5) "JESUS" COMPLAINS ABOUT THE NIGHT OF HIS BIRTH

Creating considerable controversy and confusion, the "Jesus" of *Jesus Calling* said he was born "under appalling conditions" in a "filthy stable" and that the night of his birth "was a dark night" for him. To many readers, this does not sound like the voice of their Savior—it sounds like the voice of a stranger (John 10:5) and that Satan—not Jesus—would be the one describing the night of Jesus' birth as "that dark night for Me."

THE DAMAGE CONTROL

Compare the original December 25th message with the one that has replaced it in the 10th anniversary edition of Jesus Calling. Notice how the controversial statement—"That was a dark night for Me"—was deleted and quietly replaced by the less controversial statement—"There was nothing glorious about that setting."

- **December 25th Sentence in the Original Edition**
  Try to imagine what I gave up when I came into your world as a baby. I set aside My Glory, so that I could identify with mankind. I accepted the limitations of infancy under the most appalling conditions—a filthy stable. **That was a dark night for Me**, even though angels lit up the sky proclaiming "Glory!" to awe-struck shepherds.[25] (bold added to highlight what was deleted))

- **December 25th Replacement Sentence**
  Try to imagine what I gave up when I came into your world as a baby. I set aside My Glory, so that I could identify with mankind. I accepted the limitations of infancy under the most appalling conditions—a filthy stable. **There was nothing glorious about that setting**, though angels lit up the sky proclaiming, "Glory!" to awe-struck shepherds.[26] (bold added to highlight what was added)

JESUS CORRECTS HIMSELF AGAIN?

THE complaints made by Sarah Young's "Jesus" don't square with Scripture inspired by the true Jesus Christ. The Bible tells us "to be content" in whatever circumstances we find ourselves (Philippians 4:11). Obviously succumbing to the mounting criticism regarding the "dark night for Me" remark, Sarah Young's "Jesus" corrects himself—again—with no apology or explanation.

SUMMARY

INTRIGUED by the channeled messages of *God Calling*, Sarah Young was apparently not satisfied with the sufficiency of God's Word. In her original introduction, Young stated: "I knew that God communicated with me through the Bible, but I yearned for more."[27] While this statement—along with many others—has been deleted in recent editions, it is clear the author of *Jesus Calling* "yearned for more," and more is what she got. As a result, she received "messages" from a "Jesus" that has proven himself to be one of the false Christs that the real Jesus Christ warned us would come in His name (Matthew 24:4-5, 23-24). Wanting a word from God more than the Word of God, Sarah Young ended up getting deceived. "Deceiving, and being deceived" (2 Timothy 3:13), she has taken millions of *Jesus Calling* readers along with her.

The Bible describes those who love and respect the power and authority of God's Word as those who tremble at God's Word (Isaiah 66:2). The Bible also describes those who do not tremble at God's Word but rather use and manipulate God's Word for their own selfish purposes (2 Corinthians 4:2).

There is no nice way to say it. *Jesus Calling* is a gross affront to our true Lord and Savior Jesus Christ. And the self-serving effort by Sarah Young and her publisher to cover up some of the many problems found in *Jesus Calling* is a gross affront to the body of Christ. It is one thing for Sarah Young to be deceived—it is quite another for her to be an author of deception herself.

The five examples provided in this booklet typify the unprincipled damage control that the author and her publisher have undertaken to preserve their multi-million dollar *Jesus Calling* industry—all at the expense of people who have put their trust in Sarah Young and her "Jesus." To those who would argue that there is a lot of truth in *Jesus Calling* and that the book has comforted many people, former Moody Memorial Church pastor Dr. Harry Ironside warned that "truth mixed with error is equivalent to all error, except that it is more innocent looking and, therefore, more dangerous":

Error is like leaven, of which we read, "A little leaven leaveneth the whole lump." Truth mixed with error is equivalent to all error, except that it is more innocent looking and, therefore, more dangerous. God hates such a mixture! Any error, or truth-and-error mixture, calls for definite exposure and repudiation. To condone such is to be unfaithful to God and His Word and treacherous to imperiled souls for whom Christ died.[28]

Jesus warned that great deception would characterize the time of the end and that the deception would come in His name. I am absolutely convinced that the "Jesus" of *Jesus Calling* is not the true Christ. Rather he is one of the false Christs that the real Jesus warned us to watch out for.

And as he sat upon the mount of Olives, the disciples came unto him privately, saying, Tell us, when shall these things be? and what shall be the sign of thy coming, and of the end of the world? And Jesus answered and said unto them, Take heed that no man deceive you. For many shall come in my name, saying, I am Christ; and shall deceive many. (Matthew 24:3-5)

THE NEW AGE IMPLICATIONS OF *JESUS CALLING*

IN THIS BOOK, I have described many of the problems regarding Sarah Young's best-selling book *Jesus Calling*. In particular, there are some serious New Age implications to what her "Jesus" is presenting in his "messages" to Young and her countless readers. Nevertheless, Laura Minchew, a senior vice-president at Thomas Nelson publishers, adamantly defends *Jesus Calling* and defiantly denies that the book has any New Age implications. She told *World Net Daily*, "I will tell you that should anyone hint of New Age teachings in *Jesus Calling*, they would be sorely misinformed.[1]

But Minchew's statement is both ironic and untrue. It is ironic because even as she was issuing her denial, Thomas Nelson editors were busy deleting some of the very New Age material in question. I'm not sure what Laura Minchew's understanding of the New Age is, but as a former New Ager, I can assure you there are many New Age implications—both direct and indirect—in *Jesus Calling*. In this booklet, I am going to present ten of them.

New Age Implications: Ten Examples

1) THE NEW AGE BOOK *GOD CALLING*

In an interview with the Christian Broadcasting Network, Sarah Young said she was inspired to receive "messages" from "Jesus" after reading the book *God Calling*. She stated:

> My journey began with a devotional book (*God Calling*) written in the 1930s by two women who practiced waiting in God's Presence, writing the messages they received as they "listened." About a year after I started reading this book, I began to wonder if I too could receive messages during my times of communing with God. . . . So I decided to "listen" to God with pen in hand, writing down whatever I sensed He was saying.[2]

Unfortunately, Sarah Young and her Thomas Nelson editors missed the fact that *God Calling* is a channeled New Age book. The "messages" received by the two women appear to be legitimate to the undiscerning reader because they are presented in the form of a daily devotional. Ironically, *God Calling* could have been titled *Jesus Calling* because its messages were reputedly dictated by "The Living Christ Himself."[3] It is worth noting that *Jesus Calling* is similarly titled and similarly presents its reputed "messages" from "Jesus" in the form of a daily devotional.

In *The Encyclopedia of New Age Beliefs* published by Harvest House Christian publishers, authors John Weldon and John Ankerberg provide ample evidence as to why *God Calling* is a channeled New Age book. In their chapter on channeling—under the subheading of "Impersonations of Christianity"—the two respected apologists describe *God Calling* as a book "replete with denials of biblical teaching"[4] as it "subtly encourages psychic development and spiritistic inspiration under the guise of Christ's personal guidance . . . and often misinterprets Scripture."[5] Citing a number of passages in *God*

Calling that are unbiblical and have New Age implications, the two authors explain that channeling is a form of occult mediumship and according to the Bible "is a practice forbidden (Deuteronomy 18:9-12)."[6] Yet Sarah Young stated it was *God Calling* that inspired her to receive her own "messages" from "Jesus." In her original introduction to *Jesus Calling*, Young went out of her way to praise *God Calling* as "a treasure to me."[7] Sadly, her lofty endorsement greatly popularized this New Age book within mainstream Christianity. As a result, *God Calling* is now commonly found in great numbers in various editions in both secular and Christian bookstores. In fact, it is often shelved alongside *Jesus Calling*.

Note: Young's only response to criticism of *God Calling* has been to quietly remove all her previous references to *God Calling* from the new editions of *Jesus Calling*. No explanations. No apologies. No anything. Like the missing 18½ minutes from Richard Nixon's Watergate tapes, *God Calling* has disappeared from the pages of Young's book.

2) CHANNELED "MESSAGES" FROM "JESUS"

Ruth Graham, writing about *Jesus Calling* in *The Daily Beast*—a popular online news organization formerly associated with *Newsweek* magazine—reported that Thomas Nelson had specifically requested that she not use the word "channeling" to describe how Sarah Young was receiving her "messages" from "Jesus." Graham wrote:

> Thomas Nelson specifically requested I not use the word "channeling" to describe Young's first-person writing in the voice of Jesus—the word has New Age connotations—but it's hard to avoid it in describing the book's rhetorical approach.[8]

In *Jesus Calling*, Young writes that "Jesus" told her "to be a channel of My loving Presence."[9] Obliging his request, her book is filled with channeled "messages" and "directives" she claims to have received from God. In her original introduction, she wrote:

> I have continued to receive *personal messages from God* as I meditate on Him. The more difficult my life circumstances, the more I need these *encouraging directives from my Creator.*[10] (emphasis added)

Regarding this type of spiritualism, *Webster's New World Dictionary* defines the word "channel" as follows: "to serve as a medium for (a spirit)."[11] It defines the word "directive" as "a general instruction or order issued authoritatively."[12] And by Sarah Young's own description in her original introduction, this is exactly what she is doing—being "a channel" for "encouraging directives" from a spiritual "Presence" that presents itself as "Jesus." After receiving these "messages" and "directives," she arranged them in the form of a daily devotional—just like *God Calling*.

Note: The paragraph cited above—where Young originally described how she has "continued to receive personal messages from God" and "encouraging directives" from her "Creator"—has been completely removed from the new editions of *Jesus Calling*.[13]

3) VISUALIZATION

Sarah Young engaged in the occult/New Age practice of "visualization" when she "pictured" her family "encircled by God's protective Presence":

> One morning as I prayed, *I visualized* God protecting each of us. *I pictured* first our daughter, then our son, and then Steve encircled by God's protective Presence, which looked like golden light. When I prayed for myself, I was suddenly enveloped in brilliant light and profound peace. I lost all sense of time as I experienced God's Presence in this powerful way.[14] (emphasis added)

In the same *Encyclopedia of New Age Beliefs* that described *God Calling* as a channeled New Age book, a specific chapter on visualization warns about the spiritual dangers of this New Age practice:

> "Visualization" and "guided imagery" have long been recognized by sorcerers of all kinds as the most powerful and effective methodology for contacting the spirit world in order to acquire supernatural power, knowledge, and healing. Such methods are neither taught nor practiced in the Bible as helps to faith or prayer.[15]

Sarah Young just assumed that the "light" she visualized enveloping her family and herself was from God. But one cannot assume anything in regards to spiritual experiences and spiritual encounters—especially after engaging in the occult practice of visualization. Because "many false prophets are gone out into the world," we are told to "try the spirits" to see "whether they are of God (1 John 4:1). The apostle Paul warned of deceptive "seducing spirits" (1 Timothy 4:1) and how Satan can come as "an angel of light" (2 Corinthians 11:14). Also, Jesus specifically warned us to beware of a light that appears to be light but is actually darkness (Luke 11:35).

Note: Recent editions of *Jesus Calling* have attempted to subtly demystify Sarah Young's mystical New Age "prayer" process. The phrase "looked like golden light" and the trance-like sentence "I lost all sense of time as I experienced God's Presence in this powerful way" have both been deleted from recent editions of *Jesus Calling.*[16] However, even with these deletions, Young—at least for now—continues to include her visualized prayer in the newer editions of *Jesus Calling.*

4) MEDITATION

Jesus Calling readers are led to equate Sarah Young's contemplative prayer process with biblical meditation. But to "make your mind like a still pool of water" as you passively wait "to receive whatever thoughts" Young's "Jesus" may "drop into it" is much more akin to

Eastern/New Age meditation. Biblical meditation, if you will, is an active attentiveness and thinking upon Scripture. Eastern/New Age meditation is more subjective and open to spiritual suggestion. In his August 5th message, Sarah Young's "Jesus" promotes this New Age form of meditation and contemplative prayer:

> Make your mind like a still pool of water, ready to receive whatever thoughts I drop into it.[17]

Stilling and quieting one's mind may seem to be peaceful and godly, but passively stilling the mind (i.e., putting the mind in neutral) can provide an opening for seducing spirits to communicate with an undiscerning meditator—all in the name of "Jesus," "God," and the "Holy Spirit" (Ephesians 4:27, 1 Timothy 4:1, 2 Corinthians 11:4). Sarah Young describes how she receives these "thoughts" as "messages" and "directives" as she meditates on "Jesus":

> I have continued to receive personal messages from God as I *meditate* on Him. The more difficult my life circumstances, the more I need these encouraging directives from my Creator.[18] (emphasis added)

But this kind of spiritual activity is not scriptural, and it is not biblical meditation. This is Eastern/New Age meditation. This type of meditation is what New Age channelers do to make contact with the spirit world.

Note: It bears repeating that the above paragraph containing the words "meditate," "messages," and "directives" has been deleted from recent editions of *Jesus Calling*.

5) NEW AGE TERMINOLOGY

Throughout *Jesus Calling*, Sarah Young's "Jesus" casually introduces New Age terminology in his channeled messages. Not that long ago terms like co-create,[19] divine alchemy,[20] Love-Light,[21] Light-bearer,[22] supernatural plane,[23] living channel,[24] paradigm shift,[25] true self,[26] ultimate reality,[27] universal presence,[28] etc., were sure indicators of someone's metaphysical/New Age orientation. But now these terms are commonly found in "Christian" books like *Jesus Calling* and are rapidly becoming part of the everyday language of the church.

Sarah Young's "Jesus" also makes indirect reference to two of the mega best-selling New Age books of the last thirty years—Shirley MacLaine's *Out on a Limb* and M. Scott Peck's *The Road Less Traveled*. Young's "Jesus" invites her millions of readers to "go out on a limb" with him and to take "a road less traveled":

> Be willing to go out on a limb with Me.[29]

> You, however, have been called to take a "road less traveled."[30]

Note: Obviously, these two phrases can be used in other contexts. However, the true Jesus Christ is quite aware of these groundbreaking New Age books, and it defies reason that He would make any reference—direct or indirect—to these hugely popular metaphysical books. God is not the author of confusion (1 Corinthians 14:33). And He is not going to introduce anything that might stumble someone—like nonchalantly referring to two New Age books that have already stumbled the millions of people who have read them and been influenced by them (1 Corinthians 8:9).

6) DIVINE ALCHEMY

Regarding other overlapping New Age terminology in *Jesus Calling*, Sarah Young's "Jesus" states:

> I can glean Joy out of sorrow, Peace out of adversity. Only a Friend who is also the King of kings could accomplish this divine alchemy.[31]

However, the term "divine alchemy" is an ancient, mystical, occult/New Age term that raises multiple spiritual concerns. The word "occult" is defined in *Webster's New World Dictionary* as follows:

> . . . designating or of certain alleged mystic arts, such as magic, *alchemy*, astrology, etc.[32] (emphasis added)

The *Oxford Classical Dictionary* underscores the fact that the "art" of alchemy has serious New Age implications. The very first sentence of the definition states:

> *Alchemy* in antiquity was a mixture of chemical, metallurgical, and glass technology, Greek philosophy, *mystical and syncretist religion, and astrology.*[33] (emphasis added)

The same *Oxford Dictionary* explains the occult/New Age underpinnings of alchemy itself:

> The art is distinguished from the pure science of chemistry by its mixture of *mystical and magical elements* with the technology . . . Alchemy in late antiquity was born of the confluence of three streams: (1) technology . . . (2) theory . . . (3) *occult religion.*[34] (emphasis added)

By Googling divine alchemy on the Internet, one will see countless references to the occult. The term divine alchemy is frequently found in the teachings of New Age leaders such as Marianne Williamson. She uses the term divine alchemy to reference the same practice of meditation Sarah Young's "Jesus" is advocating. She writes:

> Meditation is time spent with God in silence and quiet listening. It is the time during which the Holy Spirit has a chance to enter into our minds and perform *His divine alchemy.*[35] (emphasis added)

The *Oxford Classical Dictionary* describes the origin of alchemy and how it is linked to other occult sciences:

> The inventor was said to be Hermes [Trismegistus], and *alchemy is linked with other occult sciences* in the Hermetic literature of the first three centuries A.D., along with neo-Pythagorean, Neoplatonic, and Gnostic ideas.[36] (emphasis added)

Note: Once again, it is inconceivable that the true Jesus Christ would ever use a term like divine alchemy that is so highly identified with the occult. This is yet one more troublesome New Age aspect to *Jesus Calling* and one more reason to question the validity of Sarah Young's "Jesus."

7) CO-CREATION

Sarah Young's "Jesus" also introduces the key New Age concept of "co-creation." This is a New Age evolutionary concept that falsely teaches that because man is God, he can therefore co-create with God. But man is not God.

The New Age "Christ" has a plan. He is promising the world that Armageddon can be avoided and world peace can be achieved if everyone collaborates and "co-creates" with him. Speaking through top New Age leader Barbara Marx Hubbard in her book *The Revelation*, the New Age "Christ" uses the terms co-create, co-creation, co-creative, co-creator, and co-creatorship over 100 times. This is because co-creation is a key element in the New Age Christ's counterfeit plan of salvation for Planet Earth. At one point Hubbard's "Christ" states:

> Here we are, now poised either on the brink of destruction greater than the world has ever seen—a destruction which will cripple planet Earth forever and release only the few to go on—or on the threshold of *global co-creation* wherein

each person on Earth will be attracted to participate in his or her own evolution to godliness.[37] (emphasis added)

New Age author Neale Donald Walsch has been taking spiritual dictation from his New Age "God" for many years now. Soon after the tragic events of September 11th, 2001, "God," speaking through Walsch, proclaimed that "the era of the Single Savior is over." He said:

> Yet let me make something clear. *The era of the Single Savior is over.* What is needed now is joint action, combined effort, collective *co-creation.*[38] (emphasis added)

In *Jesus Calling*, Young's "Jesus" introduces the idea of co-creation in conjunction with the term "collaborating." *Webster's New World Dictionary's* sole definition of a collaborationist is "a person who cooperates with an enemy invader."[39] Sarah Young's "Jesus" plays right into this New Age collaboration when he talks of humanity collaborating and co-creating with him:

> This is a very practical way of *collaborating* with Me. I, the Creator of the universe, have deigned to co-create with you.[40] (emphasis added)

Co-creation is a crucial New Age concept that entails the necessity of man recognizing he is God and then acting as God to affirm, visualize, envision, and to ultimately co-create with God a positive peaceful future. Thus, there is a definite overlap of terms as Sarah Young's "Jesus" similarly teaches that humanity can partner with God through the co-creation process. Barbara Marx Hubbard's New Age "Christ" refers to a future world peace that can be visualized and co-created by mankind. This co-created world peace is referred to as the "alternative to Armageddon."[41] But the prophet Jeremiah warned about a peace that seems to heal but is, in reality, no peace at all (Jeremiah 8:11).

Note: This "alternative to Armageddon" peace process is described by New Age leaders as an important part of God's Dream for the world. Not surprisingly, "God's Dream" is another New Age concept that is introduced in *Jesus Calling*.

8) GOD'S DREAM

Consistent with many of the other New Age implications contained in her channeled messages, Sarah Young's "Jesus" introduces the New Age idea of "God's Dream" in *Jesus Calling* when he states:

> I may infuse within you a dream that seems far beyond your reach.[42]

In *Jesus Calling: 365 Devotions for Kids*, the January 6th message/devotion is titled—and has "Jesus" telling the children—"Dare to Dream My Dream."[43]

"GOD'S DREAM" IS A DECEPTIVE SCHEME

THE term "God's Dream" is yet another part of the overlapping New Age language streaming into the church. God's Dream is a vague, loosely defined New Age metaphor that attempts to unify different religions and faith groups in an unbiblical effort to attain world peace. However, the true Jesus Christ warned that deception and the coming of Antichrist—not a "God's Dream" peace movement—will be what actually precedes His ultimate and glorious return (Matthew 24:3-5; 2 Thessalonians 2:1-5). The prophet Daniel warned that Antichrist will "destroy wonderfully" and "by peace he shall destroy many" (Daniel 8:24-25). In the future, what may appear to be a "wonderful" worldwide revival and a "wonderful" world peace will actually be a false revival and a false peace—the kind of peace that Daniel said will be associated with the coming of Antichrist, not the true Christ.

The New Age concept of God's Dream was introduced at least as far back as 1916 by New Age theosophists in their *Theosophical Path Magazine*.[44] Since then it has been used by numerous New Age sympathizers that include Oprah Winfrey,[45] Wayne Dyer,[46] former United Nations Indian guru Sri Chinmoy,[47] and African bishop Desmond Tutu.[48] The concept of God's Dream was introduced into the church in the 1970s by former Crystal Cathedral pastor Robert Schuller[49] and later adopted by Rick Warren,[50] Brian McLaren,[51] Joel Osteen,[52] Bruce Wilkinson,[53] Leonard Sweet,[54] and many other Christian figures. The overlap factor is very apparent when comparing statements made by Oprah Winfrey, Joel Osteen, and Sarah Young's "Jesus":

- **Oprah Winfrey:** God can dream a bigger dream for you than you can dream for yourself.[55]

- **Joel Osteen:** God's dream for your life is so much bigger than your own.[56]

- **Sarah Young's "Jesus":** Dream your biggest, most incredible dream—and then know that I am able to do far more than that, far more than you can ever ask or imagine. Allow Me to fill your mind with My dreams for you.[57]

Rick Warren, Brian McLaren, and Leonard Sweet all used the God's Dream metaphor to stress the urgency of achieving world peace—but at what compromised New Age cost?

- **Rick Warren:** This weekend, I'll begin a series of five messages on God's dream to use you globally—to literally use YOU to help change the world! I'll unveil our Global P.E.A.C.E. plan, and how God has uniquely prepared you for this moment of destiny.[58]

- **Brian McLaren:** That in itself is an act of peacemaking, because we're seeking to align our wills with God's will, our dreams with God's dream.[59]

- **Leonard Sweet:** The time to save God's Dream is now. The People to save God's Dream are you.[60]

"GOD'S DREAM" IS A FALSE DREAM

"GOD'S Dream" may seem to be inspirational and have a godly feel to it, but there is nothing in Scripture to even hint, much less substantiate, the New Age concept of God's Dream. God doesn't dream in any way, shape, manner, or form. God's Dream is definitely one of those crossover terms like "co-creation" and "divine alchemy" that attempt to "shift" everything into a New Age context and towards the universal acceptance of a New Age/New Worldview. Sarah Young's "Jesus" plays right into this clever conditioning when he introduces the concept of God's Dream in *Jesus Calling* and in no less than three of Sarah Young's other books.[61] The prophet Jeremiah warned about those who prophesy and present false dreams like God's Dream:

> Behold, I am against them that prophesy false dreams, saith the LORD, and do tell them, and cause my people to err by their lies, and by their lightness; yet I sent them not, nor commanded them: therefore they shall not profit this people at all, saith the LORD. (Jeremiah 23:32)

Note: Because so many Christian leaders have adopted the concept of God's Dream, it has become a popularly accepted "Christian" term and is now virtually indistinguishable from its New Age origins.

9) GOD "IN" EVERYTHING

The New Age teaches we are all "One" and we are all "God" because God is "in" everyone and everything. This belief is referred to as panentheism and is the foundational teaching of the New Age movement. In my 2004 book *Deceived on Purpose*, I describe how long-time New Age evangelist Benjamin Creme, speaking on behalf of the false Christ Maitreya, presents the concept of "God in everything" as the bottom line teaching of the coming New World Religion. Creme said:

> But eventually a new world religion will be inaugurated which will be a fusion and synthesis of the approach of the East and the approach of the West. The Christ will bring together, not simply Christianity and Buddhism, but the concept of God transcendent—outside of His creation— and *also the concept of God immanent in all creation—in man and all creation.*[62] (emphasis added)

But the true Jesus Christ never taught that God was a universal Presence that is "in man and all creation." He did not teach that God is "in" everything. Yet the July 8th "message" that Sarah Young said she received from her "Jesus" definitely presents this false New Age teaching:

> I am above all, as well as in all . . . [63]

The true Jesus Christ knows that the foundational false teaching of the New Age/New Worldview is the concept of immanence—God "in all." The true Christ teaches that God—in the Person of the Holy Spirit—is sent to indwell those who believe and follow Him (John 14:23). But He would never teach that God is "in man and all creation" or "in all" as Sarah Young's "Jesus" states in *Jesus Calling*.

Note: Many Scriptures refute this idea that God is "in" all—Ezekiel 28:2, Galatians 6:3, Psalm 9:20, Isaiah 31:3, John 2:24-25, etc. Psalm 39:5 makes it very clear that "every man at his best state is altogether vanity." Man is not God or a part of God because God is not universally "in" everything—God is not "in all."

10) SARAH YOUNG'S NEW AGEY MYSTICAL MOONLIGHT CONVERSION

IN the original introduction to *Jesus Calling*, Sarah Young described how it was a walk in "God's glorious creation" that led to her mystical moonlight conversion—that her "heart" was "converted" to "Jesus" when she "felt" "enveloped" by the "warm mist" of His "Presence." Her account is reminiscent of how many of us fell prey to deceptive spiritual experiences rather than heeding warnings from the Word of God about "another Jesus," "another gospel," and "another spirit." (2 Corinthians 11:4; Galatians 1:6-7; 1 Timothy 4:1). Note how Young clearly transitions right from "it was God's glorious creation that helped me open my heart to Him" into her walk in the "snowy mountains" with its "cold moonlit beauty." It is a continuous flow from one paragraph to the next. Young wrote:

> It was the intellectual integrity of Francis Schaeffer's teaching that had drawn me to that pristine place. Though the quest that had taken me there was a search for truth, *it was God's glorious creation that helped me open my heart to Him.*

> One night I found myself leaving the warmth of our cozy chalet to walk alone in the snowy mountains. I went into a deeply wooded area, feeling vulnerable and awed by cold, moonlit beauty. The air was crisp and dry, piercing to inhale. *Suddenly I felt as if a warm mist enveloped me.* I became aware of a lovely Presence, and my involuntary response was to whisper, "Sweet Jesus." *This utterance was totally uncharacteristic of me, and I was shocked to hear myself speaking so tenderly to Jesus. As I pondered this brief communication, I realized it was the response of a converted heart; at that moment I knew I belonged to Him.* This was far more than the intellectual answers for which I'd been searching. This was a relationship with the Creator of the

universe.[64] [emphasis added to indicate what has been removed from the most recent editions of *Jesus Calling*].

But after nine years of publishing the mystical conversion account above, this original account has been suddenly replaced by a different, more traditional conversion account that Young now claims to have had prior to her moonlight walk. Instead of "God's glorious creation" transitioning into her mystical moonlight conversion, now it's her new conversion account that transitions into her considerably toned down walk in the moonlight. The new account reads:

> Shortly after I settled into the home I shared with other students, I met a gifted counselor who had come from the Swiss branch of L'Abri to talk with some of us. I went into the room where she was waiting, and she told me to close the door. Before I even had time to sit down, she asked her first question: "Are you a Christian?" I answered that I wasn't sure; I wanted to be a Christian, but I didn't really understand why I needed Jesus. I thought that knowing God might be enough. Her second question was: "What can you not forgive yourself for?" This question brought me face-to-face with my sinfulness, and immediately I understood my need for Jesus—to save me from my many sins. Later, when I was alone, I asked Him to forgive all my sins and to be my Savior-God.

> One night I found myself leaving the warmth of our cozy chalet to walk alone in the snowy mountains. I went into a deeply wooded area, feeling vulnerable and awed by cold, moonlit beauty. The air was crisp and dry, piercing to inhale. After a while, I came into an open area and I stopped walking. Time seemed to stand still as I gazed around me in wonder—soaking in the beauty of this place. Suddenly I became aware of a lovely Presence with me, and my involuntary response was to whisper, "Sweet Jesus." This

experience of Jesus' Presence was far more personal than the intellectual answers for which I'd been searching. This was a relationship with the Creator of the universe—the One who is the way, the truth, and the life (John 14:6 *NKJV*)[65]

This new conversion account immediately begs the question of why Young didn't include this recent conversion account in her original writing. For nine years she described how her "heart" was "converted" in the "cold moonlit beauty" of "God's glorious creation." Now we are being told that her heart was converted previous to her walk in the moonlight after talking with a L'Abri counselor. The skeptical reader might see the author attempting to do some quick damage control—especially in light of the fact that a number of the controversial statements from her original conversion account have been completely deleted from the most recent editions of *Jesus Calling*. Gone is the original statement that transitioned to her mystical conversion—"it was God's glorious creation that helped me open my heart to Him." Gone is the "warm mist" that "enveloped" her. Gone is the "utterance" that was "totally uncharacteristic of me." Gone is her being "shocked" to hear herself "speaking so tenderly to Jesus." Gone is her realization that her "response" was that of "a converted heart." Gone is "at that moment I knew I belonged to Him." More succinctly—gone is her whole mystical moonlight conversion and gone are the New Age implications of what she actually experienced. Also gone for many of us is any real credibility for an author and publisher who are trying to edit their problems away without any explanation or apology to anyone—much less the millions of readers who read her original version.

CONCLUSION

IT seems a bit disingenuous for Thomas Nelson Vice President Laura Minchew to deny the various New Age implications of *Jesus Calling*—even as they are deleting much of the very material that substantiates the New Age implications charge. A rose by any other name is still a rose. Same with the New Age. Like an octopus that shoots ink at its perceived adversaries to cloud the waters, Minchew's attempt to intimidate critics and to dispel legitimate criticism is not credible. Laura Minchew, Sarah Young, and Thomas Nelson editors must know this or they wouldn't be removing so much controversial material from their new editions of *Jesus Calling*.

When the author and her Thomas Nelson team choose to protect their multi-million dollar *Jesus Calling* industry rather than the truth, they betray the countless readers who have put their trust in Sarah Young's "Jesus." Nevertheless, some will still say—"but there is so much truth and so much Scripture, and I was so encouraged by Sarah Young's book." Or, "Hey, so what if they changed things. They were just trying to make it right—so what's the problem? But it is a sad day when avowed Christians find themselves encouraged by a deceptive mix of truth and New Age error. And when an author and a publisher make significant changes to spiritually controversial material, they should provide some kind of explanation as to why those changes were made.

This much is for sure. The true Christ doesn't mix truth with New Age teachings. This is what a false Christ does. When asked by His disciples what would be the sign of His coming and the end of the world, the true Jesus Christ said that deception would be the sign—that many would come in His name and pretend to be Him (Matthew 24:3-5). And while this might be hard for some people to accept, His warning specifically applies to false Christs like Sarah Young's "Jesus."

10 Scriptural Reasons Jesus Calling is a Dangerous Book

> And Jesus answered and said unto them, Take heed that no man deceive you. For many shall come in my name, saying, I am Christ; and shall deceive many. (Matthew 24:4-5)

ON NOVEMBER 12, 2015, *Religion News Service* posted an article titled *"Jesus Calling* and the Policing of Theology."[1] It was a quick response to an article that reformed pastor and popular blogger Tim Challies had posted just the day before.[2] The author of the *RNS* article, Laura Turner (a regular contributor for *Christianity Today's* "Her.meneutics" blog), used her superficial criticism of Sarah Young's best-selling book, *Jesus Calling*, as a smokescreen to actually express her disapproval of people who were issuing *serious* warnings about Young's book. In a strange stab at free speech, Turner stated that "theology policing is a job best left to the Holy Spirit, and then to people who we know." But in her effort to undermine Young's critics by redefining spiritual discernment as "theology policing," she does the very thing she accuses others of doing. Her entire article is a thinly disguised attempt to "police" those who don't agree with her own take on *Jesus Calling*. After minimizing and marginalizing most of the issues that have been raised about *Jesus Calling*, Turner concludes that Young's book is "a net positive" and "has been a tool through which many people have gotten closer to God."

In her obvious endeavor to whitewash the many problems found in *Jesus Calling*, Turner is especially upset with Tim Challies. She goes out of her way to single him out and take him to task for describing *Jesus Calling* as a "dangerous" book. But in her rush to isolate and discredit Challies, she overlooks the fact that he is not alone in coming to that conclusion. There are many of us who completely agree.

NOT CAREFUL ABOUT WHAT WE READ?

THE Bible exhorts believers to be workmen who are not ashamed of what they believe because they are "rightly dividing the Word of truth" (2 Timothy 2:15). Scripture further instructs us to "search the scriptures" to see if the things being presented in a book like *Jesus Calling* are really "so" (Acts 17:11). Yet Laura Turner writes, "Should we be careful about what we read? I'm not convinced." But in taking this attitude, she does her readers a great disfavor. While everyone should be free to read *what* they want to read, what they read *should* be read very carefully with great discernment—particularly with books that bring alleged "messages" from Jesus Christ Himself. Turner's article overlooks every warning in the Bible about the *danger* of being deceived by false Christs and false teachings. While the apostle Paul expressed his "fear" that the Corinthian church *could* be deceived by false Christs (2 Corinthians 11:3-4), the true Jesus Christ warned that before His return, many *would* be deceived by false Christs (Matthew 24:3-5).

FREE AND OPEN EXCHANGE

IN an effort to support her position, Turner ironically links to an article that actually supports the complete freedom of expression that she attempts to discourage in her own article. The article she links to was excerpted from a book written by her "friend," Liberty University English professor Karen Swallow Prior. Prior frames her piece with numerous and pertinent quotes from John Milton's 1644 anti-censorship tract, *Areopagitica*. She writes that "Milton argued passionately in this treatise that the best way to counteract falsehood is not by suppressing it, but by countering it with the truth." Prior states that the crux of Milton's argument is that "truth is stronger than falsehood; falsehood prevails through the suppression of countering ideas, but truth triumphs in a free and open exchange that allows truth to shine."[3] Exactly! It is in this "free and open exchange" that Laura Turner has the right to say whatever she wants about *Jesus Calling*, but so does everyone else—even if they don't happen to be "people who we know" and even if what they are saying and believing is that *Jesus Calling* is a "dangerous" book. The following are ten scriptural reasons explaining why so many of us believe that *Jesus Calling* is, in fact, a dangerous book.

10 SCRIPTURAL REASONS

1) NEW AGE BOOK DESCRIBED AS "A TREASURE" (MATTHEW 6:21)

In 2004, in one of her rare, carefully staged interviews, Sarah Young was asked by the Christian Broadcasting Network "How did you learn to 'dialogue' with God?" She answered that it was from reading the book *God Calling*:

> My journey began with a devotional book (*God Calling*) written in the 1930s by two women who practiced waiting in God's Presence, writing the messages they received as they "listened."[4] (parenthesis hers)

Also, in the original introduction to *Jesus Calling* that stood from 2004-2013, Young specifically praised *God Calling* as "a treasure to me."[5] However, *The Encyclopedia of New Age Beliefs* published by Christian publisher Harvest House, describes *God Calling* as a channeled New Age book that was spiritually dictated by a deceptive spirit pretending to be the real Jesus Christ.[6] In their lengthy *Encyclopedia* chapter on channeling and spiritual dictation, Christian authors/apologists John Weldon and John Ankerberg explain that channeling is a form of New Age "mediumship" which the Bible clearly defines as a "forbidden" practice (Deuteronomy 18:9-12).[7] Under a subheading titled "Impersonations of Christianity," the authors describe *God Calling* as a New Age book "replete with denials of biblical teaching"[8] that "subtly encourages psychic development and spiritistic inspiration under the guise of Christ's personal guidance . . . and often misinterprets Scripture."[9]

REMOVING *GOD CALLING*

SOON after Sarah Young's endorsement of this New Age book was widely publicized in 2013,[10] all references to *God Calling* were completely removed from all subsequent printings of *Jesus Calling*. Like the missing 18 ½ minutes from Richard Nixon's Watergate tapes, *God Calling* suddenly disappeared from Young's book. There was no explanation, no apology, no anything. But what was even more disturbing than their obvious damage control, was that Young and her publisher expressed absolutely no concern for the countless people who had already read or were currently reading *God Calling* because of Young's previous endorsement. Nor was there any expressed concern that—thanks to Young—*God Calling* had been resurrected from semi-obscurity and had become a best-selling book in its own right. It was being printed in multiple editions by multiple publishers and was frequently featured alongside *Jesus Calling* in Christian bookstores and other retail outlets.

YOUNG'S SILENCE

TO this day, Sarah Young has yet to publicly renounce, much less even acknowledge, her previous involvement with and endorsement of *God Calling*. The Bible says we are to admit our mistakes—not cover them up (Psalm 32:5). And this is especially true when millions of people have been affected by those mistakes. We are to reprove and expose books like *God Calling*—not just edit them away without any explanation (Ephesians 5:11). Scripture makes it clear that in regard to issues like *God Calling*, we are to let our "yes" be "yes" and our "no" be "no" and that it is "evil" to try and avoid the matter by refusing to clarify one's position (Matthew 5:37).

THE BIBLE WARNS ABOUT WHAT WE TREASURE

THE fact remains that Sarah Young has stated that she was inspired by *God Calling* to receive her own messages from "Jesus" and described the channeled New Age book as "a treasure to me." Until she clearly specifies otherwise, we can only assume that where her treasure is, her heart is also.

> For where your treasure is, there will your heart be also. (Matthew 6:21)

2) CHANGING *JESUS CALLING* (PROVERBS 24:21)

The removal of any mention of *God Calling* from *Jesus Calling* was not an isolated incident. It was obviously part of a concerted plan to evade some of the questions being raised about the legitimacy of Young's book. For example, in all the post-2013 printings of *Jesus Calling*, what Young had originally described as "messages" she "received" from "God" were suddenly being presented as her own "writings" and "devotions." This change in wording seemed to remove any suggestion that Young was doing the same kind of channeling that is described in *God Calling*. Yet Young made it clear in her original introduction to *Jesus Calling* that this was *exactly* what she was doing.

"BE A CHANNEL"

YOUNG writes that "Jesus" told her he was "training" her "to be a channel of My loving Presence."[11] Young made it clear in her original introduction that *Jesus Calling* was comprised of the "messages" and "directives" she claimed to "receive" from "God." She wrote:

> I have continued to receive personal messages from God as I meditate on Him. The more difficult my life circumstances, the more I need these *encouraging directives from my Creator.*[12] (emphasis added)

In regard to spiritualism and someone being "a channel," *Webster's New World Dictionary* defines the word "channel" as follows—"to serve as a medium for (a spirit)."[13] The word "directive" is defined as "a general instruction or order issued authoritatively."[14] And this is what Sarah Young originally said she was doing—being "a channel" for "personal messages" and "encouraging directives" from a spiritual "Presence" that presented itself as "Jesus." After receiving these "messages" and "directives," Young arranged them in the form of a daily devotional like *God Calling*. But just as her original references to *God Calling* were edited out of all the new printings of *Jesus Calling*, so were all of her previous references to "messages" and "directives." This convenient "now you see it, now you don't" editing eliminated the entire paragraph indented and footnoted above. Thus, the original "personal messages" and "directives" she *received* from "listening to God" became her own "writings" and "devotions" she had "gleaned" from "being still" in her "quiet moments." In the two paragraphs that follow, note how the words in her original introduction were replaced by the words in her new printings.

What has been cut and pasted and inserted into her new introduction gives entirely new meaning to her "listening" process—a process that, if not for the creative editing, is identical to the occult listening process described in *God Calling*.

- **From the Original Introduction to *Jesus Calling***
This practice of listening to God has increased my intimacy with Him more than any other spiritual discipline, *so I want to share some of the messages I have received.* In many parts of the world, Christians seem to be searching for a deeper experience of Jesus' Presence and Peace. *The messages that follow* address that felt need.[15] (emphasis added)

- **From the New Introduction to *Jesus Calling***
This practice of being still in God's Presence has increased my intimacy with Him more than any other spiritual discipline, *so I want to share some of the writings I have gleaned from these quiet moments.* In many parts of the world, Christians seem to be searching for a deeper experience of Jesus' Presence and Peace. *The devotions that follow* address that felt need.[16] (emphasis added)

However, in Young's *Jesus Calling: 365 Devotions for Kids,* the word "messages"—at least as of January 2016—had yet to be removed from the children's edition. And it is in this original kid's version that Young makes it clear that her "devotions" are, in fact, "messages" that she claims to have personally "received" from "Jesus." In the introduction, she writes:

The devotions in this book are *some of the messages* I have received.[17] (emphasis added)

THE BIBLE WARNS ABOUT UNGODLY CHANGE

THE 2014 booklet, *Changing Jesus Calling: Damage Control For a False Christ,* documents some of the subtle—and not so subtle—changes that have been made to the original text of *Jesus Calling* by Young and her team of Thomas Nelson editors.[18] It is almost unheard of that an author and a publisher would go to the seemingly unethical lengths they have to completely change the original meaning of their text—and to do so with absolutely no explanation or apology to their readers. The Bible warns us to stay away from those who are given to this kind of manipulation and change.

> My son, fear thou the LORD and the king: and meddle not with them that are given to change: For their calamity shall rise suddenly; and who knoweth the ruin of them both? (Proverbs 24:21-22)

3) SERVING TWO MASTERS (MATTHEW 6:24)

Sarah Young's "Jesus" frequently contradicts the true Jesus of the Bible. For example, in two separate messages—January 28th and October 15th—her "Jesus" states that the "last words" he spoke after his resurrection and before his final ascent to heaven were "I am with you always." But these were *not* His last words. These particular words were spoken on the Mount of Galilee as recorded in Matthew 28:16-20. His *last* words were actually spoken from the Mount of Olives as recorded in Acts 1:7-12 when He told His disciples they would be His "witnesses." It was after speaking these words that the Bible records He was "taken up" and ascended into heaven.

After these unbiblical statements in the original *Jesus Calling* were publicized in 2013,[19] Sarah Young's "Jesus" changed the wording of his two statements in a special *Jesus Calling, 10th Anniversary Edition* published in 2014.[20] Compare the original January 28th and October 15th "messages" that had been in *Jesus Calling* since 2004, with the replacement words that were inserted into the 10th anniversary edition in 2014. Notice how the two phrases "These were the last words I spoke" and "My final statement" have been removed and "after My resurrection" has been inserted in their place.

- **January 28th Statement in the Original 2004 Edition of *Jesus Calling***
I AM WITH YOU ALWAYS. These were the last words I spoke before ascending into heaven. I continue to proclaim this promise to all who will listen.[21] (emphasis added)

- **January 28th Replacement Statement in the 10th Anniversary Edition of *Jesus Calling***
I AM WITH YOU ALWAYS. I spoke these words to My disciples after My resurrection. I continue to proclaim this promise to all who will listen.[22] (emphasis added)

- **October 15th Statement in the Original 2004 Edition of *Jesus Calling***
TRY TO STAY CONSCIOUS OF ME as you go step by step through this day. My Presence with you is both a promise and a protection. *My final statement just before I ascended into heaven was: Surely I am with you always.* That promise was for all of My followers, without exception.[23] (emphasis added)

- **October 15th Replacement Statement in the 10th Anniversary Edition of *Jesus Calling***
TRY TO STAY CONSCIOUS OF ME as you go step by step through this day. My Presence with you is both a promise and a protection. *After My resurrection, I assured My followers: Surely I am with you always.* That promise was for all of My followers, without exception.[24] (emphasis added)

THE BIBLE WARNS ABOUT SERVING TWO MASTERS

THE author and her publisher might say that Young must have heard it wrong because Jesus never contradicts Himself. But if that were the case, Young would have had to hear it wrong on two separate occasions because this factually incorrect teaching is found in two separate "messages" that have distinctly different wording. Sarah Young is serving two different masters—the false Christ "Jesus" who delivers unbiblical messages like the two cited above and the Bible's Christ Jesus who she purports to be following. But the two cannot be treated as if they are the same Jesus. They can't be the same because the true Jesus does not contradict Himself and therefore has no need to correct Himself as her "Jesus" does. If Sarah Young and her readers continue to listen and hold fast to the false Christ of *Jesus Calling* and his teachings, it may be only a matter of time before this other "Jesus" gets them to despise the true Christ and His teachings.

> No man can serve two masters: for either he will hate the one, and love the other; or else he will hold to the one, and despise the other. Ye cannot serve God and mammon. (Matthew 6:24)

4) AUTHOR OF CONFUSION (1 CORINTHIANS 14:33)

The special 2014 *Jesus Calling, 10th Anniversary Edition* attempts to rectify the factually incorrect January 28th and October 15th "messages." However, the original unbiblical statements about Jesus' "last words" and "final statement" can *still* be found in all the twenty or so other varied editions of *Jesus Calling* as of January 19th, 2016. This includes the new *Jesus Calling: Morning and Evening* edition published in October 2015—published nearly a year after the corrected 10th anniversary edition.[25]

THE BIBLE WARNS THAT CONFUSION
IS NOT FROM GOD

IF all the changes, contradictions, corrections, and inconsistencies found in the various and sundry editions of *Jesus Calling* seem to be confusing—that is because they *are* confusing, and yet God's Word tells us:

> For God is not the author of confusion, but of peace, as in all churches of the saints. (1 Corinthians 14:33)

5) THE VOICE OF A STRANGER (JOHN 10:4-5)

Sarah Young's "Jesus" says he wants to be the "boss" so he can "control your mind," "reprogram your thinking," and "take full possession" as he seeks to "invade more and more areas of your life." Pray for wisdom and then ask yourself—do the following statements sound like something the true Jesus Christ would really say?

> Approach this day with awareness of *who is boss.*[26]

> Let Me *control your mind.*[27]

> My main work is to clear out debris and clutter, making room for My Spirit *to take full possession.*[28]

> Sit quietly in My Presence, letting My thoughts *reprogram your thinking.*[29]

> While you relax in My Presence, I am *molding your mind* and cleansing your heart.[30]

> Your relationship with Me is meant to be vibrant and challenging, as I *invade more and more areas of your life.*[31] (emphasis added in all the above quotes)

THE BIBLE WARNS ABOUT THE VOICE OF A STRANGER

IF truth be known, it is more likely that the Devil and his evil spirits are the ones who want to "control your mind," "take full possession," "reprogram your thinking," and "invade more and more areas of your life." The true Jesus stated that His sheep know His voice and do not follow the voice of a stranger. The voice of Sarah Young's "Jesus" is that of a stranger.

> And when he putteth forth his own sheep, he goeth before them, and the sheep follow him: for they know his voice. And a stranger will they not follow, but will flee from him: for they know not the voice of strangers. (John 10:4-5)

6) FLATTERING WORDS (1 THESSALONIANS 2:3-5)

Sarah Young's "Jesus" uses flattery to seduce undiscerning readers of *Jesus Calling*. The true Jesus Christ never used gratuitous flattery in relating to others. Pray again for wisdom and ask yourself if the following statements sound like something the real Jesus Christ would say to His followers:

> When you trustingly whisper My Name, My aching ears are soothed.[32]

> When you walk through a day in trusting dependence on Me, My aching heart is soothed.[33]

> I am aching to hold you in My everlasting arms, to enfold you in My Love.[34]

> When you seek My Face in response to My Love-call, both of us are blessed.[35]

As you listen to birds calling to one another, hear also My Love-call to you.[36]

Feel your face tingle as you bask in My Love-Light.[37]

Look into My Face and feel the warmth of My Love-Light shining upon you.[38]

When your Joy in Me meets My Joy in you, there are fireworks of heavenly ecstasy.[39]

THE BIBLE WARNS ABOUT FLATTERY

THE Bible states that "a flattering mouth worketh ruin" (Proverbs 26:28). Scripture warns of those who speak with "flattering lips" (Psalm 12:2) and that we are to have nothing to do with them (Proverbs 20:19). The prophet Daniel warned three separate times about flattery in regard to the ultimate false Christ—Antichrist. Daniel said that Antichrist would "come in peaceably" and that he would "corrupt" and "obtain the kingdom by flatteries" (Daniel 11:21, 32, 34).

> For our exhortation was not of deceit, nor of uncleanness, nor in guile: But as we were allowed of God to be put in trust with the gospel, even so we speak; not as pleasing men, but God, which trieth our hearts. For neither at any time used we flattering words, as ye know, nor a cloak of covetousness; God is witness. (1 Thessalonians 2:3-5)

7) A LOT OF LEAVEN (GALATIANS 5:9)

The New Age/New Spirituality/New Worldview teaches that we are all "One" and "we are all God" because God is "in" everyone and everything. For example, prominent New Age/New Spirituality leader Neale Donald Walsch also claims to have had conversations with God. In fact, his *Conversations with God* books have been frequent *New York Times* best-sellers. Walsch writes that "God" told him that "Oneness"—"God in everyone and everything"—is the "Foundational Truth" of a "New Spirituality" that can save the world. In regard to this heretical New Spirituality, Walsch writes:

> [W]e see God in everyone and everything. Including our divine selves.[40]

> Oneness is the message. It is the Foundational Truth of the New Spirituality.[41]

The true Jesus Christ never taught that God was "in everyone and everything." However, the July 8th "message" from Sarah Young's "Jesus" presents this same false teaching that God is "in" everything—that God is "in all." Her "Jesus" states:

> I am above all, as well as *in all*.[42] (emphasis added)

The true Jesus Christ teaches that God—in the Person of the Holy Spirit—is sent to indwell all those who truly believe and follow Him (John 14:23). But He never taught, nor would He ever teach, that He is "in" everyone and everything—that He is "in all." Psalm 39:5 makes it abundantly clear that "every man at his best state is altogether vanity." Some of the many other Bible verses that refute this false teaching that God is "in all" include Ezekiel 28:2, Galatians 6:3, Psalm 9:20, Isaiah 31:3, Romans 1:21-23, 25 and John 2:24-25.

THE BIBLE WARNS ABOUT LEAVEN

THE Bible warns that "a little leaven, leavens the whole lump," and there is more than a little leaven in Sarah Young's book. However, this particular God "in all" leaven that is in *Jesus Calling* and other "Christian" books—if left unchecked—could eventually shift the church to a New Age/New Worldview and into complete apostasy. Scripture exhorts us:

Ye did run well; who did hinder you that ye should not obey the truth? This persuasion cometh not of him that calleth you. A little leaven leaveneth the whole lump. (Galatians 5:7-9)

8) NOT TESTING THE SPIRITS (1 JOHN 4:1)

There is no indication that Sarah Young ever applied the biblical "test of the spirits" to see if the "Jesus" she claims to be getting "messages" from is the real Jesus Christ (1 John 4:1). Young references nearly a thousand Scripture verses in *Jesus Calling*, but the 1 John 4:1 test cannot be found. What is found is a completely *unbiblical* test suggested by her "Jesus." He is quoted in the March 3rd "message" of *Jesus Calling* as saying—"You must learn to discern what is My voice and what is not."[43] But instead of directing her to 1 John 4:1 and what the Bible teaches about trying and testing the spirits, he says—"Ask My Spirit to give you this discernment." This advice is not only unscriptural, it defies common sense. If the "Jesus" Sarah Young is listening to is a deceptive spirit pretending to be "Jesus," you obviously don't ask a deceptive spirit to give you discernment. If she followed his advice—which she seems to do on *all* other accounts—instead of biblically *testing* the spirit, she would already be *trusting* the deceptive spirit she should be testing. Thus, this suggestion by Sarah Young's "Jesus" is self-defeating as it immediately protects a false Christ from being detected. The fact that Young's "Jesus" teaches this unbiblical test is further proof that Sarah Young's "Jesus" is not to be trusted.

THE BIBLE WARNS TO "TRY THE SPIRITS"

Beloved, believe not every spirit, but try the spirits whether they are of God: because many false prophets are gone out into the world. Hereby know ye the Spirit of God: Every spirit that confesseth that Jesus Christ is come in the flesh is of God: And every spirit that confesseth not

that Jesus Christ is come in the flesh is not of God: and
this is that spirit of antichrist, whereof ye have heard that
it should come; and even now already is it in the world.
(1 John 4:1-3)

9) ADDING TO GOD'S WORD (PROVERBS 30:5-6)

In the original August 23rd "message" in *Jesus Calling*, Sarah Young's
"Jesus" attempts to give a new distorted description of Abraham. He
states that Abraham, in regard to his son Isaac, was guilty of "son-
worship," "undisciplined emotions," and "idolatry." Many believers
rightfully recoiled at these bizarre extra-biblical remarks. There is
nothing in the Bible to suggest that what Young's "Jesus" is saying is
in any way true. After these defamatory and derogatory references to
Abraham were widely publicized in 2013,[44] the whole Abraham and
Isaac scenario was completely removed from all subsequent printings
of *Jesus Calling*. The italicized words below show how "Abraham and
Isaac" were edited out and "Joseph and Jacob" were cut and pasted
into that otherwise same paragraph.

> • **August 23rd "Message" in the
> Original Edition (2004-2013)**
> ENTRUST YOUR LOVED ONES TO ME; release
> them into My protective care. They are much safer with
> Me than in your clinging hands. If you let a loved one
> become an idol in your heart, you endanger that one—as
> well as yourself. *Remember the extreme measures I used
> with Abraham and Isaac. I took Isaac to the very point of
> death to free Abraham from son-worship. Both Abraham and
> Isaac suffered terribly because of the father's undisciplined
> emotions.* I detest idolatry, even in the form of parental
> love.[45] (emphasis added)

- **August 23ʳᵈ Replacement Message (2014-Present)**
ENTRUST YOUR LOVED ONES TO ME; release
them into My protective care. They are much safer with
Me than in your clinging hands. If you let a loved one
become an idol in your heart, you endanger that one—
as well as yourself. *Joseph and his father, Jacob, suffered
terribly because Jacob **loved Joseph more than any of his
other sons** and treated him with special favor. So Joseph's
brothers hated him and plotted against him. Ultimately, I
used that situation for good, but both father and son had to
endure years of suffering and separation from one another.*

I detest idolatry, even in the form of parental love, so
beware of making a beloved child your idol.[46] (emphasis
added; bold is emphasis in original)

This toned-down replacement "message" from Sarah Young's
"Jesus" is yet another example of how Young and her publisher
have had her "Jesus" change his original "message" in an obvious
attempt to escape legitimate criticism.

THE BIBLE WARNS *NOT* TO ADD TO GOD'S WORD

THE original "message" depicting Abraham as a son-worshiper
and idolater was a prime example of how adding to God's Word
can end up twisting and changing God's Word. The Bible is suf-
ficient unto itself as we are "thoroughly furnished unto all good
works" (2 Timothy 3:16-17). We are clearly admonished *not* to
add to God's Word:

Every word of God is pure: he is a shield unto them
that put their trust in him. Add thou not unto his
words, lest he reprove thee, and thou be found a liar.
(Proverbs 30:5-6)

10) LAUGHING AT THE FUTURE (LUKE 6:25)

Sarah Young's "Jesus" contradicts the warnings of the true Jesus Christ in Matthew 24, Mark 13, Luke 21, and the whole Book of Revelation when he states—"The future is a phantom, seeking to spook you. Laugh at the future!"[47] In contrast, in the Bible, the true Jesus makes it clear that the future is no laughing matter. He goes to great lengths to describe the serious events that will transpire at the end of time. He tells His disciples to "be not troubled" by these future happenings, but He does not tell them to laugh at these events or to take them lightly. Rather He tells them to "watch" and "be ready" and to "not be deceived" by the false Christs and false prophets that will come in His name (Matthew 24:3-5, 24, 42, 44).

THE BIBLE WARNS ABOUT INAPPROPRIATE LAUGHTER

THE Bible says there is a "time to weep, and a time to laugh" (Ecclesiastes 3:4). The real Jesus makes it clear that the future is not something to laugh at or laugh about. Rather, He warns of the increased hatred and persecution of Christians that will be taking place—that we may even be killed for our faith. Only a false Christ would tell us to laugh at the future.

> Woe unto you that laugh now! for ye shall mourn and weep. (Luke 6:25)

CONCLUSION

FOR the above ten—and for many other scriptural reasons—it has become increasingly evident to growing numbers of believers that *Jesus Calling* is a deceptive and dangerous book. To those like Laura Turner (author of the *Religion News Service* article) who *condone* books like *Jesus Calling* as "a net positive," former Moody Memorial Church pastor Dr. Harry Ironside argued just the opposite. He reminds us there is no such thing as "a net positive" with books like

Jesus Calling. He warned that when "truth" is "mixed with error," it "is equivalent to all error, except that it is more innocent looking and, therefore, more dangerous." He said that "God hates such a mixture!" and it must be exposed and repudiated. He further warned that "to condone such is to be unfaithful to God and His Word" and "treacherous" to those "for whom Christ died."

> Error is like leaven, of which we read, "A little leaven leaveneth the whole lump." Truth mixed with error is equivalent to all error, except that it is more innocent looking and, therefore, more dangerous. God hates such a mixture! Any error, or any truth-and-error mixture, calls for definite exposure and repudiation. To condone such is to be unfaithful to God and His Word and treacherous to imperiled souls for whom Christ died.[48]

In 2 Corinthians 4:1-2, the apostle Paul was able to honestly say—"Therefore seeing we have this ministry, as we have received mercy, we faint not; But have renounced the hidden things of dishonesty, not walking in craftiness, nor handling the word of God deceitfully; but by manifestation of the truth commending ourselves to every man's conscience in the sight of God." Unfortunately, Sarah Young and Thomas Nelson cannot say the same. Through unethical editing practices, they have, in essence, made a mockery of the truth (Jeremiah 9:3). By evading legitimate questions regarding their best-selling book, they have fallen victim to covetousness and greed, coveting what was best for continued book sales but not what was best for the church (Luke 12:15). In short, they pleased themselves—not God (Galatians 1:10). With feigned words and clever editing, they have made merchandise of their trusting readers.

> And through covetousness shall they with feigned words make merchandise of you. (2 Peter 2:3)

Jesus warned that great deception would characterize the last days and that the deception would come in His Name. The "Jesus" of *Jesus Calling* is not the true Christ. He is actually one of the false Christs that the real Jesus warned us to watch out for. For that reason—and that reason alone—*Jesus Calling* is a dangerous book.

> For there shall arise false Christs, and false prophets, and shall show great signs and wonders; insomuch that, if it were possible, they shall deceive the very elect. (Matthew 24:24)

SERIOUS CONCERNS ABOUT THE *JESUS CALLING DEVOTIONAL BIBLE*

ONE OF THE many spin-off products from Sarah Young's best-selling book, *Jesus Calling*, is the *Jesus Calling Devotional Bible*. It is a *New King James Bible* filled with "messages" Young claims to have "received" from Jesus Christ. In the original introduction to her book, *Jesus Calling*, Young describes the nature of these messages:

> My journaling had changed from monologue to dialogue. Soon, messages began to flow more freely, and I bought a special notebook to record these words. [1]

> I have continued to receive personal messages from God as I meditate on Him. [2]

> This practice of listening to God has increased my intimacy with Him more than any other spiritual discipline, so I want to share some of the messages I have received. [3]

In the Introduction to Young's *Jesus Calling Devotional Bible*, she describes the "joy of listening to Jesus with pen in hand":

After many years of writing in prayer journals—and then discovering the joy of listening to Jesus with "pen in hand" —I believe all of this more than ever today.[4]

She describes the difference that this "listening to Jesus" has made in her life. She writes:

What has made the difference? The practice of listening to Jesus and letting Him speak to me. This practice has done more to increase my intimacy with Him than any other spiritual discipline. And the words of assurance and instruction that He has "spoken" to me over the years are what I have shared in my devotional books.[5]

YOUNG BELIEVES HER "MESSAGES" FROM "JESUS" BELONG IN THE BIBLE?

YOUNG'S personal "messages" from "Jesus" occupy some 250 separate full pages of her Jesus Calling Devotional Bible. Young claims that the placement of her messages and writings alongside Scripture is a "natural place" for them—and that she feels honored to have them there:

Since my writings are rooted in the infallible, unchanging Word of God, having them appear alongside the biblical text would seem to be a natural place for them. It is an honor to have devotionals from two of my books, *Jesus Calling* and *Jesus Lives*, included in this volume.[6]

However, as I pointed out in *"Another Jesus" Calling,* many of Sarah Young's "messages" in *Jesus Calling* are clearly not rooted in the "infallible, unchanging Word of God." And now, a number of these problematic "messages" have been placed throughout the pages of her *Jesus Calling Devotional Bible.*

Take, for example, the bizarre account she reputedly received from Jesus regarding Abraham and Isaac. This "message" has been placed "alongside" the actual Genesis 22 account, with her "Jesus" purportedly describing Abraham as an idolater and son-worshiper:

> Remember the extreme measures I used with Abraham and Isaac. I took Isaac to the very point of death to free Abraham from son-worship. Both Abraham and Isaac suffered terribly because of the father's undisciplined emotions. I detest idolatry even in the form of parental love.[7]

But this extrabiblical "message" from Young's "Jesus" is blatantly unbiblical. In fact, her publisher, Thomas Nelson, has removed it from some recent printings of *Jesus Calling* and related products. The original Abraham and Isaac August 23rd "devotion" has been cut and pasted and toned down to now read Jacob and Joseph rather than Abraham and Isaac. Sarah Young and her Thomas Nelson editors have removed controversial materials from recently printed *Jesus Calling* items with no explanation, apology, or repentance to Young's millions of readers. However—at least as of this writing—this original Abraham and Isaac account can still be found—unbelievably—in Young's *Jesus Calling Devotional Bible*.

Ironically, the *Jesus Calling: 365 Devotional For Kids* also keeps Abraham and Isaac in the August 23rd account. However, Young—with help from others—has cleaned up the original account to make it more biblical. The new sanitized version, according to the book's title page, originated with Sarah Young. It was adapted by a woman named Tama Fortner and then further edited by another woman named Kris Bears. And now gone is Abraham's idolatry. Gone are his undisciplined emotions. And instead of having been a son-worshiper, now he is only in danger of worshiping his son. This carefully paraphrased, adapted, and further edited version of "Jesus'" original "message" now reads:

> Abraham had waited so long for a son. When Isaac finally came, Abraham was in danger of worshipping his son. I

tested Abraham, and—as hard as it was—Abraham trusted Me to take care of Isaac. And I did.[8]

With all of this cutting, pasting, adapting, and editing away of problematic words and passages—all in the name of "Jesus"—one cannot help wonder if this is Thomas Nelson's attempt to stay one step ahead of unsuspecting readers and legitimate criticism. Responding truthfully and forthrightly about the many controversial questions surrounding Sarah Young's inconsistent "Jesus" appear to be less important than preserving her #1 best-selling book *Jesus Calling* and its many related products—like the *Jesus Calling Devotional Bible*.

OTHER PROBLEMS WITH THE *JESUS CALLING DEVOTIONAL BIBLE*

OTHER problematic "messages" contained in the original, unedited *Jesus Calling* can also be found in Young's *Jesus Calling Devotional Bible*. Perhaps the most obviously unscriptural is how Young's "Jesus" contradicts the Bible's Jesus in regards to the last words Jesus spoke before ascending into heaven. In the *Jesus Calling Devotional Bible*, with Matthew 28:20 cited at the bottom of the page, Young's "Jesus" states:

> My final statement just before I ascended into heaven was: Surely I am with you always. That promise was for all my followers, without exception.

But these were not Jesus Christ's last words. This Matthew 28:20 passage was uttered on a mount in Galilee (Matthew 28:16) while His last words were actually spoken later in Acts 1:7-9 on the Mount of Olives (Acts 1:12):

> And he said unto them, It is not for you to know the times or the seasons, which the Father hath put in his own power. But ye shall receive power, after that the Holy Ghost is come upon

you: and ye shall be witnesses unto me both in Jerusalem, and in all Judea, and in Samaria, and unto the uttermost part of the earth. And when he had spoken these things, while they beheld, he was taken up; and a cloud received him out of their sight.

Jesus is the way, the truth, and the life (John 14:6), and the true Jesus does not contradict Himself regarding His last words before ascending into heaven or any other matter. Nor does He put forth untrue, disparaging remarks about Abraham and Isaac. While it is not the purpose of this article to catalog all the concerns that arise when reading Sarah Young's *Jesus Calling Devotional Bible*, these two examples alone should be enough to keep any sincere believer far away from the *Jesus Calling Devotional Bible*.

BIBLE WARNINGS

For if he that cometh preacheth another Jesus, whom we have not preached, or if ye receive another spirit, which ye have not received, or another gospel, which ye have not accepted, ye might well bear with him. (2 Corinthians 11:4)

For the time will come when they will not endure sound doctrine; but after their own lusts shall they heap to themselves teachers, having itching ears; And they shall turn away their ears from the truth, and shall be turned unto fables. (2 Timothy 4:3-4)

Ye did run well; who did hinder you that ye should not obey the truth? This persuasion cometh not of him that calleth you. A little leaven leaveneth the whole lump. (Galatians 5:7-9)

For many shall come in my name, saying I am Christ, and shall deceive many. (Matthew 24:5)

Ten Basic Warnings About Deception

1) The true Jesus Christ said that spiritual deception would be the predominant sign at the end of the world.

> And as he sat upon the mount of Olives, the disciples came unto him privately, saying, Tell us, when shall these things be? and what shall be the sign of thy coming, and of the end of the world? And Jesus answered and said unto them, Take heed that no man deceive you. (Matthew 24:3-4)

2) The true Jesus Christ warned that false Christs would come in His name, and many people would be deceived.

> For many shall come in my name, saying, I am Christ; and shall deceive many. (Matthew 24:5)

3) Jesus Christ also warned there would be false prophets and false Christs who would work great signs and wonders (and provide

spiritual experiences) that were not from God and that, if possible, would deceive even the elect.

> Then if any man shall say unto you, Lo, here is Christ, or there; believe it not. For there shall arise false Christs, and false prophets, and shall shew great signs and wonders; insomuch that, if it were possible, they shall deceive the very elect. Behold, I have told you before. (Matthew 24:23-25)

4) The Bible warns of many being deceived in these last days by seducing spirits.

> Now the Spirit speaketh expressly, that in the latter times some shall depart from the faith, giving heed to seducing spirits, and doctrines of devils. (1 Timothy 4:1)

5) The Bible warns of hypocritical "believers" who speak out of both sides of their mouth. They are those who are described as double-tongued (1 Timothy 3:8), double-minded (James 1:8), double-hearted (Psalm 12:2)—who serve two masters (Matthew 6:24).

> He answered and said unto them, Well hath Esaias prophesied of you hypocrites, as it is written, This people honoureth me with their lips, but their heart is far from me. (Mark 7:6)

> No man can serve two masters: for either he will hate the one, and love the other; or else he will hold to the one, and despise the other. Ye cannot serve God and mammon. (Matthew 6:24)

6) There is a form of Christianity that appears to be Christian, but it is not.

> Having a form of godliness, but denying the power thereof: from such turn away. (2 Timothy 3:5)

7) The Bible warns of spiritual counterfeits that substitute good for evil, darkness for light, bitter for sweet.

> Woe unto them that call evil good, and good evil;
> that put darkness for light, and light for darkness; that
> put bitter for sweet, and sweet for bitter! (Isaiah 5:20)

> Take heed therefore that the light which is in thee be not darkness. (Luke 11:35)

8) The Bible warns of false apostles and deceitful workers in the church, of how Satan can appear as an angel of light and his ministers as ministers of righteousness.

> For such are false apostles, deceitful workers, transforming themselves into the apostles of Christ. And no marvel; for Satan himself is transformed into an angel of light. Therefore it is no great thing if his ministers also be transformed as the ministers of righteousness; whose end shall be according to their works. (2 Corinthians 11:13-15)

9) Beware of false prophets and false brethren who have crept into the church.

> For there are certain men crept in unawares, who were before of old ordained to this condemnation, ungodly men, turning the grace of our God into lasciviousness, and denying the only Lord God, and our Lord Jesus Christ. (Jude 1:4)

Beware of false prophets, which come to you in sheep's clothing, but inwardly they are ravening wolves. Ye shall know them by their fruits. (Matthew 7:15-16)

10) Know that the true Jesus Christ warned the way to eternal life is narrow and few will find it.

Enter ye in at the strait gate: for wide is the gate, and broad is the way, that leadeth to destruction, and many there be which go in thereat: Because strait is the gate, and narrow is the way, which leadeth unto life, and few there be that find it. (Matthew 7:13:14)

Ten Ways to be More Discerning

1) Be sure you are in the true faith following the one true God of Abraham, Isaac, and Jacob and the one true Savior Jesus Christ of Nazareth.

> Examine yourselves, whether ye be in the faith; prove your own selves. Know ye not your own selves, how that Jesus Christ is in you, except ye be reprobates? (2 Corinthians 13:5)

2) Measure everything by the Word of God.

> These were more noble than those in Thessalonica, in that they received the word with all readiness of mind, and searched the scriptures daily, whether those things were so. (Acts 17:11)

> Study to shew thyself approved unto God, a workman that needeth not to be ashamed, rightly dividing the word of truth. (2 Timothy 2:15)

All scripture is given by inspiration of God, and is profitable for doctrine, for reproof, for correction, for instruction in righteousness: That the man of God may be perfect, thoroughly furnished unto all good works. (2 Timothy 3:16-17)

3) Don't be ignorant of our Adversary's schemes and devices. Be sober. Be vigilant. Be prayerful. Be watchful.

Lest Satan should get an advantage of us: for we are not ignorant of his devices. (2 Corinthians 2:11)

Be sober, be vigilant; because your adversary the devil, as a roaring lion, walketh about, seeking whom he may devour. (1 Peter 5:8)

Watch and pray, that ye enter not into temptation: the spirit indeed is willing, but the flesh is weak. (Matthew 26:41)

4) Pray for discernment. Ask the one true God—as did Solomon— for spiritual discernment to help you determine good from bad, right from wrong, truth from deception.

Give therefore thy servant an understanding heart to judge thy people, that I may discern between good and bad. (1 Kings 3:9)

5) Do not seek signs and wonders and spiritual experiences.

And he [the true Jesus Christ] sighed deeply in his spirit, and saith, Why doth this generation seek after a sign? verily I say unto you, There shall no sign be given unto this generation. (Mark 8:12)

6) Do not get involved with undiscerning believers who are listening to and heeding deceptive spirits (consulting with familiar spirits).

> Regard not them that have familiar spirits, neither seek after wizards, to be defiled by them: I am the LORD your God. (Leviticus 19:31)

> There shall not be found among you...a consulter with familiar spirits, or a wizard, or a necromancer. For all that do these things are an abomination unto the LORD: and because of these abominations the LORD thy God doth drive them out from before thee. (Deuteronomy 18:10-12)

7) If you are confronted with a spiritual presence, test that spirit (1 John 4:1) and pray for discernment and wisdom from God (James 1:5). You may also, by faith, ask God to take the presence away if it is not from Him "because greater is he that is in you, than he that is in the world" (1 John 4:4).

> Beloved, believe not every spirit, but try the spirits whether they are of God: because many false prophets are gone out into the world. Hereby know ye the Spirit of God: Every spirit that confesseth that Jesus Christ is come in the flesh is of God: And every spirit that confesseth not that Jesus Christ is come in the flesh is not of God: and this is that spirit of antichrist, whereof ye have heard that it should come; and even now already is it in the world. (1 John 4:1-3)

> If any of you lack wisdom, let him ask of God, that giveth to all men liberally, and upbraideth not; and it shall be given him. But let him ask in faith, nothing wavering. For he that wavereth is like a wave of the sea driven with the wind and tossed. For let not that man think that he shall receive any thing of the Lord. (James 1:5-7)

8) If you are confronted with a person, a prophet, or a spiritual presence that tells you things that are true or that come true, but then tells you to follow after another God—do not heed that person or presence.

> If there arise among you a prophet, or a dreamer of dreams, and giveth thee a sign or a wonder, And the sign or the wonder come to pass, whereof he spake unto thee, saying, Let us go after other gods, which thou hast not known, and let us serve them; Thou shalt not hearken unto the words of that prophet, or that dreamer of dreams: for the LORD your God proveth you, to know whether ye love the LORD your God with all your heart and with all your soul. (Deuteronomy 13:1-3)

> But though we, or an angel from heaven, preach any other gospel unto you than that which we have preached unto you, let him be accursed. (Galatians 1:8)

9) Love the truth. Be valiant for the truth. The Bible warns of the consequences concerning those who do not have a love of the truth. They can become deceived and fall away.

> Even him, whose coming is after the working of Satan with all power and signs and lying wonders, And with all deceivableness of unrighteousness in them that perish; because they received not the love of the truth, that they might be saved. And for this cause God shall send them strong delusion, that they should believe a lie: That they all might be damned who believed not the truth, but had pleasure in unrighteousness. (2 Thessalonians 2:9-12)

10) Gird up the loins of your mind. Take every thought captive for Christ. Fight the good fight. Contend for the faith. Let God's truth continually preserve you.

> Wherefore gird up the loins of your mind, be sober, and hope to the end for the grace that is to be brought unto you at the revelation of Jesus Christ. (1 Peter 1:13)

> Casting down imaginations, and every high thing that exalteth itself against the knowledge of God, and bringing into captivity every thought to the obedience of Christ. (2 Corinthians 10:5)

> Fight the good fight of faith, lay hold on eternal life. (1 Timothy 6:12)

> Beloved, when I gave all diligence to write unto you of the common salvation, it was needful for me to write unto you, and exhort you that ye should earnestly contend for the faith which was once delivered unto the saints. (Jude 1:3)

> Teach me thy way, O LORD; I will walk in thy truth. (Psalm 86:11)

> O LORD: let thy lovingkindness and thy truth continually preserve me. (Psalm 40:11)

THE GOSPEL
OF THE TRUE
JESUS CHRIST

Jesus saith unto him, I am the way, the truth, and the life: no man cometh unto the Father, but by me. (John 14:6)

1) The true Jesus Christ said we must be born again from above.

That which is born of the flesh is flesh; and that which is born of the Spirit is spirit. Marvel not that I said unto thee, Ye must be born again. (John 3:6-7)

2) To be born again we must recognize we are lost, fall short of the glory of God, and are sinners.

And he said, That which cometh out of the man, that defileth the man. For from within, out of the heart of men, proceed evil thoughts, adulteries, fornications, murders, thefts, covetousness, wickedness, deceit, lasciviousness, an evil eye, blasphemy, pride, foolishness: all these evil things come from within, and defile the man. (Mark 7:20-23)

For all have sinned, and come short of the glory of God. (Romans 3:23)

3) To remain in our sin is spiritual death. Believing in Jesus Christ brings eternal life and is a gift from God.

Jesus said unto her, I am the resurrection, and the life: he that believeth in me, though he were dead, yet shall he live. (John 11:25)

For the wages of sin is death; but the gift of God is eternal life through Jesus Christ our Lord. (Romans 6:23)

4) To save us from our sin, God sent His Son Jesus Christ to be our Savior.

For God so loved the world, that he gave his only begotten Son, that whosoever believeth in him should not perish, but have everlasting life. For God sent not his Son into the world to condemn the world; but that the world through him might be saved. (John 3:16-17)

5) The true Jesus Christ said we must repent of our sins.

I tell you, Nay: but, except ye repent, ye shall all likewise perish. (Luke 13:3)

6) To save us from our sin, Jesus Christ died for our sins on the Cross of Calvary.

But God commendeth his love toward us, in that, while we were yet sinners, Christ died for us. (Romans 5:8)

7) On the Cross of Calvary, Jesus Christ defeated sin and death.

Forasmuch then as the children are partakers of flesh and
blood, he also himself likewise took part of the same; that
through death he might destroy him that had the power of
death, that is, the devil. (Hebrews 2:14)

**8) If you confess with your mouth and believe in your heart that
Jesus Christ is Lord and that God raised Him from the dead you
will be saved.**

That if thou shalt confess with thy mouth the Lord Jesus,
and shalt believe in thine heart that God hath raised him
from the dead, thou shalt be saved. (Romans 10:9)

**9) We are saved by God's grace through Jesus Christ—not by our
own works.**

For by grace are ye saved through faith; and that not of
yourselves: it is the gift of God: Not of works, lest any man
should boast. (Ephesians 2:8-9)

10) True faith comes from hearing the Word of God.

So then faith cometh by hearing, and hearing by the word
of God. (Romans 10:17)

**11) Because of faith in the finished work of the true Jesus Christ on
the Cross, we have peace with God.**

Therefore being justified by faith, we have peace with God
through our Lord Jesus Christ. (Romans 5:1)

12) We are the children of God by faith in Jesus Christ's work of redemption on the Cross.

> For ye are all the children of God by faith in Christ Jesus. (Galatians 3:26)

13) If we believe in the true Jesus Christ and continue in His Word, then we are His disciples.

> Then said Jesus to those Jews which believed on him, If ye continue in my word, then are ye my disciples indeed; And ye shall know the truth, and the truth shall make you free. (John 8:31)

14) The apostle Paul emphasized that we must stand on the truth and keep the Gospel of the true Jesus Christ.

> Moreover, brethren, I declare unto you the gospel which I preached unto you, which also ye have received, and wherein ye stand; by which also ye are saved, if ye keep in memory what I preached unto you, unless ye have believed in vain. For I delivered unto you first of all that which I also received, how that Christ died for our sins according to the scriptures; and that he was buried, and that he rose again the third day according to the scriptures. (1 Corinthians 15:1-4)

15) Whoever calls upon the Lord in sincerity and truth will be saved.

> For whosoever shall call upon the name of the Lord shall be saved. (Romans 10:13)

***If you have never repented of your sins and asked the true Jesus Christ to be your Lord and Savior, consider doing it right now while it is still day—because night is coming on fast.

ENDNOTES

PROLOGUE

1. Johanna Michaelsen, *The Beautiful Side of Evil* (Eugene, OR: Harvest House Publishers, 1982), p. 154.

2. Sarah Young, *Jesus Calling: Enjoying Peace in His Presence* (Nashville, TN: Thomas Nelson, 2004), pp. VII-VIII.

3. Ibid., p. VIII.

4. Ibid., p. XI.

PART ONE: *GOD CALLING*

1. CHANNELED BOOK FROM JESUS?

1. Two Listeners; Edited by A. J. Russell, *God Calling* (Grand Rapids, MI: A Spire Book published by Jove Publications Inc., for Fleming H. Revell, 2005), p. 5.

2. Sarah Young, *Jesus Calling*, op. cit., pp. XI-XII.

3. Q & A with Sarah Young, Author Profile, The Christian Broadcasting Network (http://www.cbn.com/entertainment/books/JesusCallingQA.aspx).

4. John Ankerberg & John Weldon, *Encyclopedia of New Age Beliefs* (Eugene, OR: Harvest House Publishers, 1996), p. 80.

5. Ibid., p. 103.

6. Ibid., p. 104.

7. Two Listeners, *God Calling*, op. cit., p. 145.

8. Ibid., p. 29.

9. Ibid., p. 17.

10. Ibid., p. 53.

2. PERMEATED WITH NEW AGE TERMINOLOGY

1. Two Listeners, *God Calling*, op. cit., p. 19.

2. Ibid., p. 141.

3. Ibid., p. 42.

4. Ibid., p. 36.

5. Ibid., p. 42.

6. Ibid., p. 171.

7. Ibid., p. 167.

8. Ibid., p. 26.

9. Ibid., p. 17.

10. Ibid., p. 78.

11. Ibid., p. 37.

12. Ibid., p. 46.

13. Ibid., p. 52.

14. Ibid., p. 33.

15. Ibid., p. 159.

16. Ibid., p. 194.

17. Ibid., p. 18.

18. Ibid., p. 155.

19. Ibid., p. 88.

20. Ibid., p. 129.

21. Ibid., p. 152.

22. Ibid., p. 23.

23. Ibid., p. 128.

3. GOD'S UNIVERSAL SPIRIT?

1. Two Listeners, *God Calling*, op. cit., p. 19.

2. Ibid., p. 49.

3. Two Listeners; Edited by A. J. Russell, *God at Eventide: Companion Volume to God Calling* (New Alresford, Great Britain: John Hunt Publishing Ltd., 1950, 1953), p. 110.

4. Sarah Young, *Jesus Calling*, op. cit., p. 175.

4. GOD "IN" EVERYONE?

1. Benjamin Creme, *The Reappearance of the Christ and the Masters of Wisdom* (London, England: The Tara Press, 1980), p. 88; Alice Bailey and Djwhal Khul, *The Reappearance of the Christ,* Chapter 6—"The New World Religion" (Caux, Switzerland: Netnews Association and/or its suppliers, 2002), (http://www.net-news.org), (http://web.archive.org/web/20070220093122/http://laluni.helloyou.

ws/netnews/bk/reappearance/reap1025.html).

2. Two Listeners, *God Calling*, op. cit., p. 55.

3. Ibid., p. 88.

5. NAME IT & CLAIM IT

1. Two Listeners, *God Calling*, op. cit., p. 63.

2. Ibid., p. 91.

3. Ibid., p. 57.

4. Ibid., p. 83.

5. Ibid., p. 23.

6. Ibid., p. 26.

7. Ibid., p. 205.

8. Ibid., p. 26.

9. Ibid., pp. 131, 146, 175, 194. Cited here are four direct references. There are numerous general references as well.

6. EXPERIENCE REPLACES GOD'S WORD

1. Two Listeners, *God Calling*, op. cit., p. 12.

2. Ibid., p. 184.

3. Ibid., p. 76.

4. *A Course in Miracles: Combined Volume*, Second Edition (Glen Ellen, CA: Foundation for Inner Peace, 1975, 1992, Manual for Teachers), p. 77.

5. Ibid. (Workbook), p. 398.

6. Neale Donald Walsch, *Conversations with God: an uncommon dialogue*, Book 1 (New York, NY: G.P. Putnam's Sons, Hardcover Edition 1996), p. 8.

7. JESUS NEEDS US MORE THAN WE NEED HIM?

1. Two Listeners, *God Calling*, op. cit., p. 60.

2. Two Listeners, *God at Eventide*, op. cit., p. 126.

3. Two Listeners, *God Calling*, op. cit., pp. 75-76.

8. NEW TRUTH & NEW REVELATION?

1. Two Listeners, *God Calling*, op. cit., p. 26.

2. Ibid., p. 43.

3. Ibid., p. 22.

4. Ibid.

5. Two Listeners, *God at Eventide*, op. cit., p. 176.

6. Ibid.

7. Ibid., p. 181.

8. Ibid., p. 145.

9. Ibid., p. 165.

9. THE NEW AGE & PSALM 46:10

1. Two Listeners, *God Calling*, op. cit., p. 19.

2. Deepak Chopra, *The Seven Spiritual Laws of Success: A Practical Guide to the Fulfillment of Your Dreams* (San Rafael, CA: Co-published by Amber-Allen Publishing and New World Library, 1994), p. 14.

3. Ibid., pp. 16-17.

4. Ken Blanchard & Phil Hodges, *Lead Like Jesus: Lessons from the Greatest Leadership Role Model of All Time* (Nashville, TN: W Publishing Group, a division of Thomas Nelson Publishers, 2005), pp. 160-161.

10. NEW AGE CHRISTIANITY?

1. Two Listeners, *God Calling*, op. cit., p. 55.

PART TWO: *JESUS CALLING*

1. INSPIRED BY A CHANNELED NEW AGE BOOK

1. Sarah Young, *Jesus Calling*, op. cit., pp. XI-XII.

2. CHANNELING JESUS?

1. Sarah Young, *Jesus Calling*, op. cit., p. 94.

2. Ibid., p. 303.

3. Ibid., p. 318.

3. TEST THE SPIRITS

1. Sarah Young, *Jesus Calling*, op. cit., p. 66.

2. Ibid.

4. JESUS CONTRADICTS HIMSELF?
1. Sarah Young, *Jesus Calling*, op. cit., p. 29. With thanks to Steve Griffith.
2. Pastor Larry DeBruyn e-mail sent to author on subject.

5. JESUS TELLS US TO LAUGH AT THE FUTURE?
1. Sarah Young, *Jesus Calling*, op. cit., p. 16.
2. *A Course in Miracles: Combined Volume* (Teacher's Manual), op. cit., p. 37.

6. THE FLATTERY OF JESUS?
1. Sarah Young, *Jesus Calling*, op. cit., p. 203.
2. Ibid., p. 182.
3. Ibid., p. 216.
4. Ibid., p. 262.
5. Ibid., p. 377.
6. Ibid., p. 310.
7. Ibid., p. 239.
8. Ibid., p. 278.
9. Ibid., p. 199.
10. Ibid., p. 139.

7. *WHO* WANTS US TO REST BY THE WAYSIDE?
1. Sarah Young, *Jesus Calling*, op. cit., p. 228.
2. Two Listeners, *God at Eventide*, op. cit., pp. 120-121.
3. Sarah Young, *Jesus Calling*, op. cit., p. 228.
4. *A Course in Miracles: Combined Volume* (Manual for Teachers), op. cit., p. 87.
5. Barbara Marx Hubbard, *The Revelation: A Message of Hope for the New Millennium* (Novato, CA: Nataraj Publishing, 1995), p. 202.

8. VISUALIZING JESUS?
1. Dave Hunt & T.A. McMahon, *The Seduction Of Christianity: Spiritual Discernment in the Last Days* (Eugene, OR: Harvest House Publishers, 1985), p. 123. See also John Ankerberg & John Weldon, *Encyclopedia of New Age Beliefs*, op. cit., p. 578.
2. Sarah Young, *Jesus Calling*, op. cit., pp. VIII-IX.

3. Ibid., pp. X-XI.

4. Warren B. Smith, *The Light That Was Dark: From the New Age to Amazing Grace* (Magalia, CA: Mountain Stream Press, 2005), pp. 16-17.

5. Ophiel, *The Art and Practice of Getting Material Things Through Creative Visualization* (San Francisco, CA: Peach Publishing Company, 1968), p. i. With thanks to Danny Frigulti for this source.

6. Ibid., p. 1.

9. THE DARK NIGHT OF JESUS' BIRTH?

1. Sarah Young, *Jesus Calling*, op. cit., p. 376.

10. ABRAHAM GUILTY OF "IDOLATRY" & "SON-WORSHIP"?

1. Sarah Young, *Jesus Calling*, op. cit., p. 246.

2. Matthew Henry, *Matthew Henry's Commentary on the Whole Bible* (Peabody, MA: Hendrickson Publishers Inc., 1991), p. 53.

11. CONTEMPLATIVE PRAYER, THE NEW AGE, & PSALM 46:10

1. Sarah Young, *Jesus Calling*, op. cit., p. 306.

2. Ibid., p. 228.

3. Ibid., p. 200.

4. Ibid., p. 116.

5. Two Listeners, *God Calling*, op. cit., p. 84.

6. Sarah Young, *Jesus Calling*, op. cit., p. 189.

7. Two Listeners, *God Calling*, op. cit., p. 19.

8. Alice Bailey and Djwhal Khul, *A Treatise on White Magic, Rule Four—The Creative Work of Sound* (Caux, Switzerland: Netnews Association and/or its suppliers, 2002; http://www.netnews.org; http://web.archive.org/web/20060225030003/http://laluni.helloyou.ws/netnews/bk/magic/magi1055.html).

9. *A Course in Miracles: Combined Volume* (Text), op. cit., p. 52.

10. The Findhorn Community, *The Findhorn Garden: Pioneering a New Vision of Man and Nature in Cooperation* (New York, NY: Harper & Row Publishers, 1975), p. 36.

11. Ibid.

12. Ibid., pp. 36-37.

13. Matthew Henry, *Matthew Henry's Commentary on the Whole Bible*, op. cit., p. 810.

14. Sarah Young, *Jesus Calling*, op. cit., p. 258.

15. Ibid., p. XIII.

16. Two Listeners, *God Calling*, op. cit., p. 60.

17. Larry DeBruyn, "Who Goes There? (Guarding His Flock Ministries, http://guardinghisflock.com/2010/11/16/who-goes-there-2).

12. PRACTICING *WHAT* PRESENCE?

1. Joel S. Goldsmith, *Practicing the Presence* (New York, NY: HarperOne, 1958, 1991), p. 74.

2. Ibid., p. 46.

3. Ibid., p. 135.

4. Ibid., p. 96.

5. Tamara Hartzell, *"Reimagining" God: Turning the Light off to Look for "Truth" in the Corner of a Dark Round Room, Volume 2*, (North Charleston, SC: CreateSpace, an Amazon company, 2013), pp. 394-395. For endnote documentation throughout, see her book which is also posted online: http://www.inthenameofpurpose.org/ReimaginingGod.pdf).

6. Sarah Young, *Jesus Calling*, op. cit., p. 367.

7. Ibid., p. 5.

8. Sarah Young, *Jesus Today: Experience Hope Through His Presence* (Nashville, TN: Thomas Nelson, 2012), p. 122.

9. *Catechism of the Catholic Church* (New York, NY: Doubleday, 1995), p. 228.

10. Ibid., p. 129.

11. Ibid.

12. Brother Lawrence, *The Practice of the Presence of God with Spiritual Maxims* (Grand Rapids, MI: Spire Books, a division of Baker Publishing Group, 1958, 1967), pp. 70-71.

13. Ibid., pp. 72-73.

14. Two Listeners, *God Calling*, op. cit., p. 55.

15. Joel S. Goldsmith, *Practicing the Presence*, op. cit., p. 74.

13. "CO-CREATING" WITH GOD

1. Victoria Neufeldt, Editor in Chief, *Webster's New World Dictionary* (New

York, NY: Simon & Schuster., Inc 1988, Third College Ed.), p. 273.

2. Sarah Young, *Jesus Calling*, op. cit., p. 362.

3. Neale Donald Walsch, *The New Revelations: A Conversation with God* (New York, NY: Atria Books, 2002), p. 157.

4. Barbara Marx Hubbard, *The Revelation*, op. cit., p. 174.

5. Ibid., pp. 312-313.

6. Tamara Hartzell, *"Reimagining" God*, op. cit., pp. 408-409.

7. Barbara Marx Hubbard, *The Revelation,* op. cit., p. 245.

8. Ibid., p. 111.

9. Ibid., p. 197.

10. Tamara Hartzell, *"Reimagining" God*, op. cit., p. 406.

14. Quantum Leap, Quantum "Christ"

1. Sarah Young, *Jesus Calling*, op. cit., p. 285.

2. Barbara Marx Hubbard, *The Revelation*, op. cit., p. 111.

3. Ibid., p. 261.

4. Ibid., pp. 316-317.

5. Sarah Young, *Jesus Calling*, op. cit., p. 285.

6. William P. Young, *The Shack: Where Tragedy Confronts Eternity* (Newbury Park, CA: Windblown Media, 2007), p. 95.

7. Ibid., p. 112.

8. Sarah Young, *Jesus Calling*, op. cit., p. 363.

9. Ibid., p. 314.

10. Annette Capps, *Quantum Faith* (England, AR: Capps Publishing, 2003, 2007), p. 4.

11. Sarah Young, *Jesus Calling*, op. cit., p. 199.

15. "Cocoon of Light"

1. Barbara Marx Hubbard, *The Revelation*, op. cit., p. 309; cited by Tamara Hartzell, *"Reimagining" God*, op. cit., pp. 406-407.

2. Ibid.

3. Hubbard, *The Revelation*, op. cit., p. 228.

4. Ibid., p. 176.

5. Sarah Young, *Jesus Calling*, op. cit., p. 166.

6. Ibid., p. 362.

16. The "Great Work" of "Divine Alchemy"

1. Sarah Young, *Jesus Calling*, op. cit., p. 260.

2. *Webster's New World Dictionary*, Third College Ed., p. 937.

3. Edited by N. G. L. Hammond and H. H. Scullard, *The Oxford Classical Dictionary* (Oxford, UK: Oxford University Press, Second Edition, 1970), p. 36.

4. Ibid. pp. 36-37.

5. Ibid., p. 37.

6. Marianne Williamson, *A Return to Love: Reflections on the Principles of A Course in Miracles* (New York, NY: Harper Perennial, 1996), p. 281.

7. Barbara Marx Hubbard, *The Revelation*, op. cit., p. 147.

8. Ibid., p. 203.

9. *The Oxford Classical Dictionary*, op. cit., p. 36.

10. Two Listeners, *God Calling*, op. cit., pp. 71, 78.

11. Marianne Williamson, *Healing the Soul of America: Reclaiming Our Voices as Spiritual Citizens* (New York, NY: Simon&Schuster, 1997, 2000), p. 195.

12. *Messages from Maitreya the Christ: One Hundred Forty Messages* (Los Angeles, CA: Share International Foundation, Second Edition, 1980, Second Printing 2001), p. 142.

13. Two Listeners, *God Calling*, op. cit., p. 17.

14. Ibid., pp. 27, 37.

15. Sarah Young, *Jesus Calling*, op. cit., p. 94.

16. Ibid., p. 260.

17. Jesus is Above All & "in" All?

1. Sarah Young, *Jesus Calling*, op. cit., p. 199.

2. Benjamin Creme, *The Reappearance of the Christ and the Masters of Wisdom* (London, England: The Tara Press, 1980), p. 88. Cited from Warren B. Smith, *Deceived on Purpose* (Magalia, CA: Mountain Stream Press, 2nd ed., 2004), p. 156.

3. Alice Bailey and Djwhal Khul, *The Reappearance of the Christ*, Chapter 6—"The New World Religion" (http://www.netnews.org), (http://web.archive.org/web/20070220093122/http://laluni.helloyou.ws/netnews/bk/reappearance/reap1025.html).

4. Ronald S. Miller and the Editors of *New Age Journal*, *As Above, So*

Below: Paths to Spiritual Renewal in Daily Life (Los Angeles, CA: Jeremy P. Tarcher, Inc., 1992), p. xi.

18. MOVING TOWARD A NEW AGE/NEW WORLDVIEW

1. M. Scott Peck, *The Road Less Traveled: A New Psychology of Love, Traditional Values and Spiritual Growth* (New York, NY: Simon & Schuster, 1978), p. 281.

2. Shirley MacLaine, *Out on a Limb* (New York, NY: Bantam Books, 1983, 1984), p. 347.

3. Sarah Young, *Jesus Calling*, op. cit., p. 313.

4. Ibid., p. 360.

5. Ibid., p. 209.

6. Ibid., p. 5.

7. Ibid., p. 139.

8. Ibid., p. 214.

9. Ibid., p. 241.

10. Ibid., p. 303.

11. Ibid., p. 260.

12. Ibid., p. 362.

13. Ibid., p. 85.

14. Ibid., p. 381.

15. Sarah Young, *Jesus Today*, op. cit., p. 46.

16. Esther Hicks, *Law of Attraction: The Basics of the Teachings of Abraham* (Carlsbad, CA: Hay House, Inc., 2006), p. 18.

17. *Webster's New World Dictionary*, op. cit., p. 50.

18. Sarah Young, *Jesus Calling*, op. cit., p. 166.

19. Barbara Marx Hubbard, *The Revelation*, op. cit., p. 228.

20. Sarah Young, *Jesus Calling*, op. cit., p. 152.

21. William Wordsworth, "Lines Composed a Few Miles Above Tintern Abbey," *Treasury of Favorite Poems*, Edited by Louis Untermeyer, (New York, NY: Barnes & Noble, Inc., 1932, 1996), line 152, p. 211.

22. Ibid., William Wordsworth, "The World is Too Much With Us," p. 213.

23. Ibid., William Wordsworth, "Lines Composed a Few Miles Above Tintern Abbey," lines 93-94, 100-102, p. 209.

24. Sarah Young, *Jesus Calling*, op. cit., p. 367.

25. Ibid., p. 5.

26. Ibid., p. 199.
27. Ibid., p. 196.

19. Would Jesus Magnify His Presence Above the Word of God?

1. Sarah Young, *Jesus Calling*, op. cit., p. 234.
2. Ibid., p. 187.
3. Ibid., p. 233.
4. Ibid., p. 3.
5. Ibid., p. 13.
6. Ibid., p.135.
7. Ibid,. p. 352.
8. Two Listeners, *God Calling*, op. cit., p. 43.
9. Ibid., p. 21.
10. Sarah Young, *Jesus Calling*, op. cit., p. 314.
11. Ibid., p. 189.
12. Sarah Young, *Jesus Calling*, op. cit., pp. XI-XII.

20. "Another Jesus" Calling

1. Dr. Harry Ironside, "Exposing Error: Is it Worthwhile?" (*TBC Extra*, April 2008, posted on The Berean Call website, http://www.thebereancall.org/content/tbc-extra-30).
2. This young woman's written account was personally given to Tamara Hartzell. It is reprinted here with the young woman's permission.
3. Transcribed by Tamara Hartzell as this young woman spoke them to her. Reprinted here with the young woman's permission.
4. Sarah Young, *Jesus Calling*, op. cit., p. 143.
5. Ibid., p. 116.
6. Ibid., p. 200.
7. Ibid., p. 50.
8. Ibid., p. 132.
9. Ibid., p. 16.
10. Ibid., p. 183.

Epilogue

1. *A Course in Miracles: Combined Volume* (Workbook), op. cit., p. 222.

2. Rabindranath R. Maharaj with Dave Hunt, *Death of a Guru: A Hindu Comes to Christ* (New York, NY: A. J. Holman Company: Division of J. B. Lippincott Company, 1977), pp. 219-220.

3. Barbara Marx Hubbard, *The Revelation*, op. cit., pp. 40-42.

4. Ibid., p. 55.

5. Ibid., p. 64.

6. Ibid., p. 63.

7. Ibid., p. 64.

8. Ibid.

9. Ibid., pp. 288-291.

APPENDIX A

1. Two Listeners; Edited by A.J. Russell, *God Calling*, op. cit., p. 5.

2. Q&A with Sarah Young, Author Profile, The Christian Broadcasting Network (http://www.cbn.com/entertainment/books/JesusCallingQA.aspx).

3. Two Listeners, *God Calling*, op. cit., p. 5.

4. John Ankerberg & John Weldon, *Encyclopedia of New Age Beliefs,* op. cit., p. 80.

5. Ibid., p. 103.

6. Ibid., p. 104.

7. Sarah Young, *Jesus Calling: Enjoying Peace in His Presence* (Nashville, TN; Thomas Nelson, 2004), p. Xl, (12 13 14 15 16 RRD 52 51 50 49 48).

8. Ruth Graham, "The Strange Saga of '*Jesus Calling*,' The Evangelical Bestseller You've Never Heard Of" (*Daily Beast,* 02/23/14, http://www.thedailybeast.com/articles/2014/02/23/the-strange-saga-of-jesus-calling-the-evangelical-bestseller-you-ve-never-heard-of.html).

9. Ibid.

10. Jim Fletcher, "Top Christian Bestseller Accused of Heresy" (*WorldNetDaily*, http://www.wnd.com/2014/05/top-christian-bestseller-accused-of-heresy).

11. Jim Fletcher, "Is Hit Book '*Jesus Calling*' Pushing New Age?" (*WorldNetDaily* (http://www.wnd.com/2014/06/is-hit-book-jesus-calling-pushing-new-age).

12. Gina Meeks, "Critics Accuse '*Jesus Calling*' of Mixing Truth With New Age Error" (*Charisma News*, http://www.charismanews.com/culture/43855-critics-accuse-jesus-calling-of-mixing-truth-with-error).

13. Sarah Young, *Jesus Calling*, op. cit., p. Xlll.

14. Sarah Young, *Jesus Calling: Enjoying Peace in His Presence*, 10th Anniversary Edition (Nashville, TN; Thomas Nelson Inc, 2004, 2011, 2014), p. xviii, (14 15 16 17 18 DSC 5 4 3 2 1).

15. Sarah Young, *Jesus Calling*, op. cit., p. XlV.

16. Sarah Young, *Jesus Calling*, 10th Anniversary Edition, op. cit., p. xix.

17. Sarah Young, Adapted by Tama Fortner, Edited by Kris Bearss, *Jesus Calling for Kids: 365 Devotions for Kids* (Nashville, TN; Tommy Nelson, 2010), pp. vii-viii, (13 14 15 16 17 RRD 5 4 3 2 1).

18. Sarah Young, *Jesus Calling*, op. cit., p. 29.

19. Sarah Young, *Jesus Calling*, 10th Anniversary Edition, op. cit., p. 29.

20. Sarah Young, *Jesus Calling*, op. cit., p. 302.

21. Sarah Young, *Jesus Calling*, 10th Anniversary Edition, op. cit., p. 302.

22. Sarah Young, *Jesus Calling Devotional Bible* (Nashville, TN; Thomas Nelson, 2011), p. vi, (11 12 13 14 15 16 17 18—RRD—8 7 6 5 4 3 2 1).

23. Sarah Young, *Jesus Calling*, op. cit., p. 246.

24. Sarah Young, *Jesus Calling* 10th Anniversary Edition, op. cit., p. 246.

25. Sarah Young, *Jesus Calling*, op. cit., p. 376.

26. Sarah Young, *Jesus Calling*, 10th Anniversary Edition, op. cit., p. 376.

27. Sarah Young, *Jesus Calling*, op. cit., p. Xll.

28. Dr. Harry Ironside, "Exposing Error: Is it Worthwhile?" (TBC Extra, April 2008, posted on The Berean Call website, http://www.thebereancall.org/content/tbc-extra-30).

APPENDIX B

1. Jim Fletcher, "Top Christian Bestseller Accused of Heresy" (World Net Daily, http://www.wnd.com/2014/05/top-christian-bestseller-accused-of-heresy).

2. Q&A with Sarah Young, Author Profile (The Christian Broadcasting Network http://www.cbn.com/entertainment/books/jesuscallingqa.aspx).

3. Two Listeners, *God Calling*, op. cit., p. 5.

4. John Ankerberg & John Weldon, *Encyclopedia of New Age Beliefs,* op. cit., p. 103.

5. Ibid., p. 104.

6. Ibid., p. 80.

7. Sarah Young, *Jesus Calling: Enjoying Peace in His Presence* (Nashville,

TN; Thomas Nelson, 2004), pp. Xl-XII, Printing 12 13 14 15 RRD 49 48 47 46.

8. Ruth Graham, "The Strange Saga of '*Jesus Calling*,' The Evangelical Bestseller You've Never Heard Of" (*The Daily Beast*, 02/23/14), http://www. thedailybeast.com/articles/2014/02/23/the-strange-saga-of-jesus-calling-the-evangelical-bestseller-you-ve-never-heard-of.html).

9. Sarah Young, *Jesus Calling,* op. cit., p. 94.

10. Ibid., p. Xll.

11. Victoria Neufeldt, Editor in Chief, *Webster's New World Dictionary: Third College Edition* (New York, NY: Simon & Schuster, Inc. 1988), p. 234.

12. Ibid., p. 389.

13. Sarah Young, *Jesus Calling;* 10th Anniversary Edition (Nashville, TN; Thomas Nelson Inc, 2004, 2011, 2014), Printing 14 15 16 17 18 DSC 5 4 3 2 1.

14. Sarah Young, *Jesus Calling*, op. cit., pp. X-Xl.

15. John Ankerberg & John Weldon, *Encyclopedia of New Age Beliefs*, op. cit., p. 578. Quoted from Dave Hunt & T.A. McMahon, *The Seduction of Christianity: Spiritual Discernment in the Last Days* (Eugene, OR: Harvest House Publishers, 1985), p. 123.

16. Sarah Young, *Jesus Calling,* 10th Anniversary Edition, op. cit.

17. Sarah Young, *Jesus Calling,* op. cit., p. 228.

18. Ibid., p. Xll.

19. Ibid., p. 362.

20. Ibid., p. 260.

21. Ibid., p. 139.

22. Ibid., p. 214.

23. Ibid., p. 241.

24. Ibid., p. 303.

25. Ibid., p. 85.

26. Ibid., p. 381.

27. Ibid., p. 209.

28. Ibid., p. 5.

29. Ibid., p. 360.

30. Ibid., p. 313.

31. Sarah Young, *Jesus Calling*, op. cit., p. 260.

32. *Webster's New World Dictionary;* Third College Edition, op. cit., p. 937.

33. Edited by N.G.L. Hammond and H.H.Scullard, *The Oxford Classical*

Dictionary, op., cit., p. 36.

34. Ibid., pp. 36-37.

35. Marianne Williamson, *A Return to Love: Reflections on the Principles of A Course in Miracles* (New York, NY: Harper Perennial, 1996), p. 281.

36. Edited by N.G.L. Hammond and H.H. Scullard, *The Oxford Classical Dictionary*, op. cit., p. 37.

37. Barbara Marx Hubbard, *The Revelation: A Message of Hope for the New Millennium* (Novato, CA: Nataraj Publishing, 1995), p. 174.

38. Neale Donald Walsch, *The New Revelations: A Conversation with God* (New York, NY: Atria Books, 2002), p. 157.

39. Victoria Neufeldt, Editor in Chief, *Webster's New World Dictionary*, Third College Edition, op. cit., p. 273.

40. Sarah Young, *Jesus Calling*, op. cit., p. 362.

41. Barbara Marx Hubbard, *The Revelation*, op. cit., p. 264.

42. Sarah Young, *Jesus Calling*, op. cit., p. 6.

43. Sarah Young (adapted by Tama Fortner), *Jesus Calling: 365 Devotions For Kids* (Nashville, TN: Tommy Nelson, 2010), p. 7.

44. Katherine Tingley, Editor, *Theosophical Path Magazine*, Volume X, February 1916, p. 159.

45. Ann Oldenburg, "The Divine Miss Winfrey" (*USA Today*, May 10, 2006, http://www.usatoday.com/life/people/2006-05-10-oprah_x.htm).

46. Wayne Dyer, *You'll See it When You Believe It: The Way to Your Personal Transformation* (New York, N.Y.: HarperCollins, First Quill Ed., 2001), p. 108.

47. Sri Chinmoy; late resident Indian guru at the United Nations (http://www.yogaofsrichinmoy.com/god_the_author_all_good/mangod).

48. Desmond Tutu, "Archbishop Desmond Tutu Speech" (March 18, 2004, Bender Arena at American University, http://wwwl.media,american.edu/speeches/desmondtutu.htm).

49. Robert H. Schuller, *Your Church Has Real Possibilities* (Glendale, CA: Regal Books Division, G/L Publications, 1974), pp. 176-179.

50. Rick Warren, Saddleback Church e-mail, October 27, 2003, "GOD'S DREAM FOR YOU—AND THE WORLD!"; Warren Smith, *Deceived on Purpose: The New Age Implications of the Purpose-Driven Church* (Magalia, CA: Mountain Stream Press, 2004), pp. 131-142.

51. Brian McLaren, *The Secret Message of Jesus: Uncovering the Truth that Could Change Everything* (Nashville, TN: W. Publishing Group, a Division

of Thomas Nelson, Inc., 2006), p. 161.

52. Joel Osteen, "God's Dream for Your Life"—Joel Osteen Ministries daily devotional 28 July Monday" (http://devotion.wedaretobelieve. com/2014/07/gods-dream-for-your-life-joel-osteen.html).

53. Bruce Wilkinson, *The Dream Giver* (Sisters, OR: Multnomah Publishers, Inc., 2003), p. 77.

54. Leonard Sweet, *SoulTsunami: Sink or Swim in the New Millennium Culture* (Grand Rapids, MI: Zondervan, 1999), p. 34.

55. Ann Oldenburg, "The Divine Miss Winfrey" (*USA Today,* May 10, 2006, http://www.usatoday.com/life/people/2006-05-10-oprah_x.htm).

56. Joel Osteen, "God's Dream for Your Life (Joel Osteen Ministries daily devotional 28 July 2014").

57. Sarah Young (adapted by Tama Fortner), *Jesus Calling: 365 Devotions For Kids*, op. cit. p. 7.

58. Rick Warren, Saddleback Church e-mail, October 27, 2003, "GOD'S DREAM FOR YOU—AND THE WORLD!"; op. cit.

59. Brian McLaren, *The Secret Message of Jesus,* op cit., p. 161.

60. Leonard Sweet, *SoulTsunami,* op. cit., p. 34.

61. Sarah Young, *Dear Jesus: Seeking His Light in Your Life* (Nashville, TN: Thomas Nelson, Inc., 2007), pp. 68-69; Sarah Young: *Jesus Lives: Seeing His Love in Your Life* (Nashville, TN: Thomas Nelson, 2009), p. 124; Sarah Young (adapted by Tama Fortner), *Jesus Calling: 365 Devotions For Kids*, op. cit., p. 7.

62. a) Benjamin Creme, *The Reappearance of the Christ and the Masters of Wisdom* (London, England: The Tara Press, 1980), p. 88, Cited from *Deceived on Purpose* (Magalia, CA: Mountain Stream Press, 2nd ed., 2004), p. 156. b) Alice Bailey and Djwhal Khul, *The Reappearance of the Christ*, Chapter 6—"The New World Religion" (Caux, Switzerland: Netnews Association and/or its suppliers, 2002), http://netnews.org), http://web.archive.org/ web/20070220093122/http://laluni.helloyou.ws/netnews/bk/reappearance/ reap1025.html).

63. Sarah Young, *Jesus Calling,* op. cit., p. 199.

64. Sarah Young, *Jesus Calling* (original introduction), op. cit., pp. Vll-Vlll.

65. Sarah Young, *Jesus Calling* (revised introduction), (10th Anniversary Edition), op. cit., p. xiv.

APPENDIX C

1. Laura Turner, "*Jesus Calling* and the Policing of Theology" (Religion News Service, November 12, 2015; http://lauraturner.religionnews.com/2015/11/12/jesus-calling-and-the-policing-of-theology/).

2. Tim Challies, "10 Serious Problems with *Jesus Calling*" (November 11, 2015, http://www.challies.com/articles/10-serious-problems-with-jesus-calling).

3. Karen Swallow Prior, "Promiscuous Reading" (Posted at The Well, an InterVarsity online outreach to women, http://thewell.intervarsity.org/arts-books-media/promiscuous-reading).

4. "Q&A with Sarah Young, Author Profile" (The Christian Broadcasting Network, http://www.cbn.com/entertainment/books/jesuscallingqa.aspx).

5. Sarah Young, *Jesus Calling: Enjoying Peace in His Presence* (Nashville, TN; Thomas Nelson, 2004), p. Xl (12 13 14 15 16 RRD 52 51 50 49 48).

6. John Ankerberg & John Weldon, *Encyclopedia of New Age Beliefs,* op. cit., pp. 79-112.

7. Ibid., p. 80.

8. Ibid., p. 103.

9. Ibid., p. 104.

10. Warren B. Smith, *"Another Jesus" Calling: How False Christs are Entering the Church Through Contemplative Prayer* (Eureka, MT; Lighthouse Trails Publishing, 2013), pp. 24-26, 52-53.

11. Sarah Young, *Jesus Calling*, op. cit., p. 94.

12. Ibid., p. Xll.

13. Victoria Neufeldt, Editor in Chief, *Webster's New World Dictionary: Third College Edition*, op. cit., p. 234.

14. Ibid., p. 389.

15. Sarah Young, *Jesus Calling*, op. cit., p. Xlll.

16. Sarah Young, *Jesus Calling: Enjoying Peace in His Presence, 10ᵗʰ Anniversary Edition* (Nashville, TN; Thomas Nelson Inc, 2004, 2011, 2014), p. xviii, (14 15 16 17 18 DSC 5 4 3 2 1).

17. Sarah Young, Adapted by Tama Fortner, Edited by Kris Bearss, *Jesus Calling: 365 Devotions for Kids* (Nashville, TN; Tommy Nelson, 2010), pp. vii-viii, (13 14 15 16 17 RRD 5 4 3 2 1).

18. Warren B. Smith, *Changing Jesus Calling: Damage Control for a False Christ* (Eureka, MT: Lighthouse Trails Publishing, 2014).

19. Warren B. Smith, *"Another Jesus" Calling,* op. cit., pp. 59-61 ("Jesus Contradicts Himself?").

20. Sarah Young, *Jesus Calling, 10th Anniversary Edition*, op. cit., pp. 29, 302.

21. Sarah Young, *Jesus Calling*, op. cit., p. 29.

22. Sarah Young, *Jesus Calling, 10th Anniversary Edition*, op. cit., p. 29.

23. Sarah Young, *Jesus Calling*, op. cit., p. 302.

24. Sarah Young, *Jesus Calling, 10th Anniversary Edition*, op. cit., p. 302.

25. Sarah Young, *Jesus Calling: Morning & Evening* (Nashville, TN: Thomas Nelson, 2015), pp. 56, 596.

26. Sarah Young, *Jesus Calling*, op. cit., p. 21.

27. Ibid., p. 116.

28. Ibid., p. 326.

29. Ibid., p. 200.

30. Ibid., p. 329.

31. Ibid., p. 50.

32. Ibid., p. 203.

33. Ibid., p. 182.

34. Ibid., p. 377.

35. Ibid., p. 239.

36. Ibid., p. 216.

37. Ibid., p. 262.

38. Ibid., p. 278.

39. Ibid., p. 199.

40. Neale Donald Walsch, *Happier than God: Turn Ordinary Life into an Extraordinary Experience* (Ashland, OR: Emnin Books, 2008), p. 207.

41. Neale Donald Walsch, *Tomorrow's God: Our Greatest Spiritual Challenge* (New York, NY: Atria Books, 2004), p. 167.

42. Sarah Young, *Jesus Calling*, op. cit., p. 199.

43. Ibid., p. 66.

44. Warren B. Smith, *"Another Jesus" Calling*, op. cit., pp. 76-79 ("Abraham Guilty of 'Idolatry' & 'Son-Worship'?").

45. Sarah Young, *Jesus Calling*, op. cit., p. 246.

46. Sarah Young, *Jesus Calling, 10th Anniversary Edition*, op. cit., p. 246.

47. Sarah Young, *Jesus Calling*, op. cit., p. 16.

48. Dr. Harry Ironside, "Exposing Error: Is it Worthwhile?" (TBC Extra, April 2008, posted on The Berean Call website, (http://www.thebereancall.org/content/tbc-extra-30).

APPENDIX D

1. Sarah Young, *Jesus Calling: Enjoying Peace in His Presence*, op. cit., p. XII in the original Introduction.

2. Ibid.

3. Ibid., p. XIII in the original Introduction.

4. Sarah Young (General Editor), *Jesus Calling Devotional Bible: Enjoying Peace in His Presence* (Nashville, TN: Thomas Nelson Inc., 2011), p. V.

5. Ibid.

6. Ibid., p. VI.

7. Ibid., p. 37.

8. Sarah Young, *Jesus Calling: 365 Devotions For Kids* (Nashville, TN: Tommy Nelson, 2010), p. 246.

9. Sarah Young, *Jesus Calling Devotional Bible*, p. 1237.

Note: Our attempts to speak with Sarah Young about the problematic issues in *Jesus Calling* have been to no avail. Thomas Nelson has repeatedly stated that she is not available for interviews.

Index

A

Abraham 8, 50, 71, 72, 73, 74, 106, 109, 140, 141, 178, 179, 184, 185, 187, 192

A Course in Miracles 34, 44, 50, 59, 63, 67, 78, 123, 124, 203, 205, 206, 209, 212

alchemy 11, 99, 100, 101, 102, 103, 109, 150, 151, 152, 153, 157

"alternative to Armageddon" 155

angels of light 66

Ankerberg, John 132, 146, 166

Antichrist 16, 54, 61, 94, 96, 105, 123, 155, 175

Armageddon 58, 89, 153, 154, 155

armour of God, 61

as above, so below 106

astrology 100, 101, 152

automatic writing 26

B

Bailey, Alice 77, 83, 105

Bears, Kris 185

biblical meditation 81, 125, 127, 149, 150, 220

Blanchard, Ken 41, 42

Note: Certain words and phrases that are used frequently in this book, such as *Jesus Calling* and New Age, are not in this Index.

D

DeBruyn, Larry 55, 56, 82
deceptive spirits 66, 75, 124
demonic spirits 63
discernment 19, 53, 193, 194
divine alchemy
       see alchemy
Divine Mind 26
doctrine 35, 86, 109, 115
Dyer, Wayne 156

E

emerging church 80
Encyclopedia of New Age Beliefs 23, 149
end times 16
esoteric mysteries 95
esoteric traditions 102
eucharist 128

F

false prophets 15, 53, 54, 56, 58, 119, 122, 140, 149, 177, 180, 188,
       189, 190, 194
familiar spirits 23
Findhorn 78
flattery 11, 61, 174, 175

G

Gawain, Shakti 67
global co-creation 90, 153
gnostic ideas 101, 153
God Calling 10-11, 20-25, 27, 29-30, 32-37, 39, 41, 44, 45, 48-50,
       59, 62, 75, 76, 80, 81, 83, 87, 99, 102-103, 115, 132-135 143,
       146-149, 165-168
God "in" everyone 96, 109
God's covenant with man 73

R

S

T

OTHER BOOKS BY WARREN B. SMITH

- *Deceived on Purpose: The New Age Implications of the Purpose-Driven Church*
- *A "Wonderful" Deception: The Further New Age Implications of the Emerging Purpose Driven Movement*
- *False Christ Coming—Does Anybody Care?: What New Age Leaders Really Have in Store for America, the Church, and the World*
- *The Light That Was Dark: From the New Age to Amazing Grace*
- *Watering the Greyhound Garden: Stories From the Streets of San Francisco*

For retail and wholesale orders, contact Bookmasters at: (877) 312-3520 and (800) 247-6553. International (419) 281-1802.

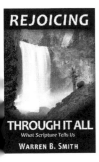

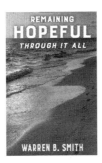

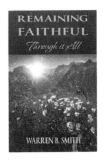

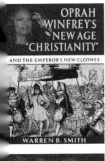

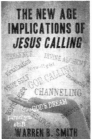

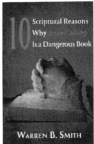

To order the above booklets, call Lighthouse Trails at (866) 876-3910
or visit www.lighthousetrails.com.

DVDs and Booklets by Warren B. Smith

DVDS

Quantum Lie: God is NOT in Everything
Three Talks in Bend, Oregon
Standing Fast in the Last Days

BOOKLETS

The New Age Implications of Jesus Calling
Changing Jesus Calling: Damage Control for a False Christ
10 Reasons Jessus Calling is a Dangerous Book
Rick Warren's Daniel Plan
The Shack and Its New Age Leaven
Remaining Hopeful Through It All
The Awesome Wonder of God's Word
Being Thankful Through It All
Praising God Through it All
Be Still and Know That You Are Not God
Truth or Consequences
False Revival Coming: Holy Laughter or Strong Delusion
Rejoicing Through It All
Blessings Through It All
Remaining Faithful Through It All
Standing Fast Through It All
Trusting God Through It All
Oprah Winfrey's New Age Christianity - Part 1
Oprah Winfrey's New Age Christianity - Part 2

Order all of the above from Lighthouse Trails (866) 876-3910. For a complete listing of Warren B. Smith's books, booklets, DVDs, and articles, visit his website at www.warrenbsmith.com.

66254295R00130

Made in the USA
Lexington, KY
08 August 2017